RITUALS FOR HERETICS

TRANSCENDENT RITES FOR ATHEISTS AND PEOPLE WHO AREN'T SURE ABOUT GOD

JEREMY STEELE

First Edition
Printed in the USA

Cover design and interior layout by Matthew J. Distefano

PAPERBACK ISBN 978-1-964252-71-1
ELECTRONIC ISBN 978-1-964252-72-8

Published by Quoir
Chico, California
www.quoir.com

CONTENTS

INTRODUCTION

This might sound weird, but your brain loves ritual.

Not just churchy ritual. Not just incense-and-incantation ritual. I'm talking about any intentional act that links your inner world with your outer behavior, like lighting a candle when you're sad, writing something down and tearing it up, tying a string around your wrist, and saying a few words to no one in particular.

Your brain? It eats that up.

Why? Because rituals are psychologically powerful.

1. They bypass your overthinking brain.

Most of us are experts at rumination. We rehearse conversations, spiral through emotions, or make endless pros-and-cons lists. But rituals move the problem into your body. They give your hands something to do. Your senses something to notice. And when you move your body with intention, your mind often follows.

It's like tricking yourself into clarity.

2. They mark the moment.

A breakup. A new job. A death. A decision. A loss you can't name but still feel in your chest.

If you don't mark these moments, they have a tendency to leak out sideways (that's the technical psychological term)—through anxiety, numbness, or unfinished grief. Rituals give your inner life a timestamp. They say: This mattered. And now... you're on the other side of it, or you're at least going to take another step forward.

3. They give your subconscious a job.

Psychologists know that when you symbolically act out a change—burning something, burying it, offering it up—your unconscious gets the message. It starts looking for closure, or healing, or courage... even while you're asleep. That's not magic. That's just how brains work.

So yeah. Rituals are good for you.

But God can be a real problem.

Most of us grew up around rituals that were loaded. Maybe they were beautiful and meaningful, or maybe they came with guilt, shame, and a side of religious trauma.

Maybe you loved them, but no longer believe the story they're tied to. Maybe you flinch a little when someone lights a candle and says, "Let us pray..."

I get it.

But here's the thing. Rituals from every major tradition—Christianity, Hinduism, Judaism, Buddhism, Indigenous ceremonies, Pagan rites—have all been used for centuries to meet deeply human needs: to let go of guilt, to start over, to grieve someone you've lost, to feel connected to something bigger, to ask for wisdom you can't find alone

But when you're outside the religious world (or healing from it), these rituals can feel inaccessible. Or worse, triggering.

That's why I wrote this book.

There's no reason you should lose out on millennia of human knowledge, innovation, and discovery because you had some pastor manipulate you out of your money. The idea in this book is to translate those practices, to make them safe, accessible, and useful even if you're not sure what you believe about God.

So I stripped out the theology—and left the transformation.

You won't find prayers to a specific deity. But you will find meaningful ways to move through the things life throws at you.

If you want to bring your own spirituality into the ritual—go for it.

If not? You'll still get all the benefits. These rituals work, with or without belief.

How to Use This Book

In the first section, you'll find a set of what you might expect from a book of rituals. They involve sensory elements, words to say, and things to think about. Each ritual is titled to help you easily identify which one suits the need or intention you're bringing into your life. Think of these titles as guideposts. They're there to help you choose the ritual that resonates most with what you're experiencing or hoping to explore.

You'll also notice that each ritual includes a bit of preparation—what you'll need to gather ahead of time and how to set your space. These steps are there to help you create a meaningful environment for each ritual and to invite you into a space of intention.

As you explore the rituals, you'll also notice that each one includes prompts for reflection and space for you to write directly in the book. These prompts invite you to jot down any adaptations you made to personalize the ritual and to reflect on what you experienced. In this way, the book becomes your own record of your journey. You can return to these pages later to remember what you felt, what you learned, and how you want to move forward.

In the second section, you'll find a collection of meditation practices. While these are also rituals, they operate a bit differently. Meditation, in this context, is about engaging the mind and allowing the subconscious to surface. Psychological research shows that meditation can help unlock deeper layers of awareness, reduce stress, and allow for a form of internal communication that many people experience as spiritual or divine. For those who are religious, this can be a way of experiencing the presence of God or a higher power. For those who are not, it can simply be a way of tuning into one's own inner wisdom.

In other words, these meditation rituals are here to offer you another layer of connection—one that's mental and emotional rather than physical. Feel free to approach them in whatever way aligns with your beliefs.

I hope this layout helps you navigate the book and find the practices that resonate with you. Enjoy exploring these rituals and making them your own.

Rituals

One

Letting Go of What Others Called You

Origins of this Ritual

There is a therapeutic mode of practice called narrative therapy. This approach sees our inner life through the lens of story. We tell a story about ourselves that comes not just from our own thoughts, but from the influences, both good and bad, that come to us from the outside world and the other characters in our lives.

Along the way, we often incorporate less-than-healthy plot lines and character traits that begin to shape how we see ourselves, taking the story of our lives in directions we may not consciously choose. The power of this approach is that when we identify those plot points and internalized attributes, we can begin to revise them by telling a new story about who we are and where we're headed.

Bringing this internal narrative into the physical world through ritual engages our senses and bodies in the act of transformation. This specific ritual focuses on the parts of our identity shaped by the negative names and labels we've received from others, labels that may still influence how we see ourselves. Through fire, a universal symbol of transformation and purification, we enact the burning away of these false identities and the invocation of our truer, self-chosen names.

Trigger Warning: Diving into these words can bring up painful memories. If you are in a hard place, pay attention to timing and emotional energy. Take care of yourself.

Ritual

Prepare:

Bring these items:

1. A number of pieces of paper

2. A writing utensil

3. Something to catch the paper on fire

4. Something to place the burning paper in that will allow it to burn out without catching other things on fire

Grounding:

1. Take a moment to center yourself. Breathe in slowly, counting to four as you breathe in. Take another four-count pause before breathing out for another count of four. Do this four times.

2. As you breathe, focus on your breath. Feel the way the air moves across your lips as it goes in. Listen to the sound of your breathing. Feel the rise and fall of your chest. Focus on those sensations to help your mind recenter and ground you.

Remembering:

1. Once grounded, turn your thoughts to your sense of who you are and pay attention to the negative names (labels count as names as well) that people have used for you, or that you may have used for yourself or internalized without consciously knowing them. They might be words like "loser," "bitch," or "entitled."

2. As they come, write them down on the left half of the paper.

Pause:

These names have had power over you. Take a moment to recognize that power and feel the weight of it as you breathe slowly in and out.

Rename:

1. Slowly look at each name you have been given and find an opposite, positive name you want to accept in its place. Don't be overly concerned with it being exactly the opposite. This is about identifying the attribute of the person you are, at your core, that pushes back against the negative name.

2. Slowly, with intention, put a line through the negative name.

3. Next to the name you just crossed out on the right-hand side of the page, write the opposite, positive name.

Re-write:

1. Once you have crossed out every name and written a new one, take out another sheet of paper.

2. Pause to look at the blank page. Remind yourself that you are starting anew. You are going to release those old names completely.

3. Then rewrite the list of the positive, new names on this page.

Burn:

1. Take the pages with the old names and light them on fire.

2. Place the paper in the container you brought, letting it burn while keeping your surroundings safe.

3. Do not burn the page or pages that hold only the new names.

Release:

1. Watch the smoke rise.

2. As the smoke rises, speak aloud the true names you claim for yourself three times, letting them become part of you.

3. Allow yourself to both speak and hear the names being spoken.

4. Imagine the old names being consumed in the fire and rising into the air with the smoke, leaving your life released into the air.

5. Take the ashes from the burning and dispose of them in the least respectful place you can easily access.

Remind:

1. Think through a typical day and week. Find a place where you spend time most days.

2. Take the page with the new names and put it in that place so you regularly see your new names.

Inhale:

1. In that space, look at the names.

2. Take deep breaths and imagine that with each breath you are taking the names deeper within yourself.

3. Walk out of the space, imagining that you are taking a new path.

Make It Yours

What changes did or could you make to the ritual to better suit your context or needs?

Reflect

What old names or labels came to mind as you began?

How did your body feel as you let go of them?

What new identity or truth felt more real afterward?

Two

Hoping Something Good Will Take Root

Origins of this Ritual

Planting seeds is one of the oldest known human practices, so ancient that it marks the very beginning of civilization. Archaeologists estimate that humans began cultivating crops and domesticating plants around 10,000 to 12,000 years ago, initiating a shift from hunter-gatherer societies to agricultural settlements. This wasn't just a change in food production; it was a transformation in how we experienced time, shaped identity, and imagined the sacred.

To plant something is to enact a behavior that has been hardwired into the human imagination for over 12,000 years. Long before written language, before temples or scrolls, humans were placing seeds into the earth with the instinctive hope that something life-giving would come forth. Planting isn't just practical; it's primal. It connects us to our ancestors and to the part of our brain that knows, deep down, that growth takes time, care, and trust in what we cannot yet see.

A seed germinates invisibly. Its roots stretch downward before anything ever emerges into the light. If nurtured—protected from weeds, harsh sun, and drought—it can grow into something nourishing, beautiful, or enduring. This image mirrors the work of inner transformation. What we plant inwardly with intention can grow, with care, into the shape of a new life.

Modern psychology echoes this ancient wisdom. Research in behavioral science and mental health shows that symbolic actions can reinforce goal-setting and increase follow-through. When a personal intention is tied to a tangible, sensory act, like planting, it becomes more real to the brain. This helps shift our mindset from wishful thinking to committed action. The act of planting externalizes hope and anchors motivation in the body.

It's no surprise, then, that planting has taken on ritual significance in religious traditions across the world. A few striking examples include:

Judaism — During Tu BiShvat, the New Year of Trees, it is customary to plant trees and eat fruits native to the land of Israel. The holiday emphasizes ecological renewal, interconnectedness, and gratitude for creation.

Hinduism — Planting a Tulsi (holy basil) plant is a sacred act in many Hindu homes. Tulsi is honored as a living goddess. Daily offerings and prayers to the plant are believed to purify the household and invite spiritual blessings.

Christianity — Rogation Days, first instituted in the 5th century by Pope Mamertus in Gaul (modern-day France), are observed with processions through fields and blessings of seeds, soil, and water. These rituals affirm humanity's dependence on divine provision and express collective prayers for protection, fertility, and a fruitful harvest.

Shinto (Japan) — Rice planting festivals, like Otaue Matsuri, feature ceremonial planting by shrine maidens, accompanied by traditional music and dance. These rituals are offerings to the kami, spiritual beings that animate the natural world, and are believed to harmonize the human and divine.

Indigenous cultures of the Americas — Among the Haudenosaunee (Iroquois Confederacy), Zuni, and Hopi peoples, planting ceremonies center on the Three Sisters: corn, beans, and squash. These crops are honored not only for their agricultural synergy but for their spiritual symbolism. Planting is accompanied by offerings to Earth Mother, songs, dances, and seasonal prayers that reflect a sacred relationship between the land, the people, and their ancestors.

This ritual draws deeply on that lineage. But instead of planting crops or trees, you will plant your most personal intentions—the things you desire to grow in your life. Just like a seed, an intention takes root in the unseen soil of your spirit. And just like a plant, it flourishes not by magic, but by patient tending.

Ritual

Prepare:

1. Get two pieces of paper and a writing utensil.

2. Find a pot with a plant in it or a place outside, under, or beside a plant where you can make a small hole.

3. Get a trowel or something to make a hole in the ground or a pot.

4. Go to a quiet place, preferably outside, where you can have a couple of moments alone.

Dream:

1. Take four box breaths: inhaling to a count of four, holding for a count of four, exhaling for a count of four, and waiting to inhale for a count of four.

2. Begin to allow yourself to dream about what you would most like to see in your life in the next month, the next six months, and the next year. These do not need to be connected, but they can.

3. Write each of them on one of the pieces of paper, and then do it again on the second piece.

Set your intention:

1. Go outside and hold the pieces of paper. Imagine these actually happening. Envision the moment they occur in the future. Who

would be there? How would you feel?

2. As you imagine the moments, fold one of the pieces of paper into a smaller size.

3. Set down the papers. Holding those images in your mind, make a hole big enough for the folded paper in the ground or pot.

Plant your intention:

1. Place the folded paper in the hole, cover it well, and continue to tend the plant over the next days, weeks, and months. When you do, reflect with hope on the dream you had for your future.

2. Place the second piece of paper in a place where you will see it occasionally. When you do, take a moment of time for hopeful reflection on your dreams.

Make It Yours

What changes did or could you make to the ritual to better suit your context or needs?

Reflect

What do these seeds represent for you?

What conditions will help them take root?

How do you want to care for what's growing?

Three

Needing to Start Over After a Mess

Origins of this Ritual

In the early centuries of Christianity, people carved out a forty-day season before Easter to take stock of their lives. It was a time to name the ways they'd gotten off course, reflect on the kind of person they still wanted to become, and begin the slow work of returning.

Some were preparing for a new identity through baptism. Others had walked away from their values, or their community, and needed a path back. But everyone was invited to reset—to strip away distraction and clear space for something deeper to take root.

They practiced this through fasting, prayer, self-reflection, and time with their sacred texts. Not as penance, but as intention.

That season began with a ritual we now call Ash Wednesday. People marked their skin with ashes—what's left when the fire has done its work. It was more than a symbol of grief or repentance. It was a reckoning with mortality. A reminder that we are made of dust, and to dust we will return.

That truth wasn't meant to shame them. It was meant to wake them up. Life is short. You won't live forever. What are you waiting for?

Ashes had long carried this weight. In the Jewish tradition that early Christians inherited, people covered themselves in ashes when they were mourning, when they were lost, when they knew something had to change. It was never about performance. It was about honesty.

And ashes don't just mean loss. They mark the end of something that no longer belongs, and the beginning of whatever comes next. That's the heart of this ritual—to name what's no longer working, to face the reality of your own impermanence, and to begin again with clarity.

Psychology gives language to what this ancient ritual intuited: confronting mortality can clarify purpose. Research in existential psychology shows that when we honestly face our finite nature—not as despair, but as truth—we often experience what's called a mortality salience effect: a sharpening of priorities, a deepened gratitude, and a renewed sense of meaning. The ashes remind us that our time is limited, and that awareness has power. It invites us to stop delaying the changes that matter and start living with intention now.

Ritual

Prepare:

Before you begin, gather a few things:

1. A quiet space where you can be alone and uninterrupted

2. Something to mark yourself with: ash, charcoal, soil, powdered spice—anything dark and earthy

3. A mirror (optional, but it can make the moment more vivid)

4. A way to write, if you'd like to capture thoughts as they come

You don't need anything fancy—just what helps you be honest.

Gather:

1. Let the quiet settle. No music. No distractions.

2. Take deep breaths and allow your heart and mind to slow.

3. When you're ready, say out loud: "This is the beginning. The beginning of returning. I want to return to the person I want to be.

I want to return to what actually matters. I want to return to the path that leads to the best version of myself."

Reflect:

1. Pause. Begin to imagine the person you want to be, the best version of yourself.

2. Remember the good things you wanted for yourself in the past.

3. Recall the good dreams you had for yourself.

4. Write them down.

5. Read this slowly: "There's a path I meant to walk. There's a version of me I've drifted from."

6. Pause to reflect on the turning points, choices, and things you have done that got you off track from the things you wanted to do and be. Write them down.

7. Continue reading slowly: "Time is not unlimited. The days of my life are not infinite. I will eventually run out of time. I don't need to wait to start again. I just need to start."

Mark yourself:

1. Choose a symbol that means God, the divine, or hope.

2. Take the ashes, charcoal, or other material you have brought. Dip your finger in them, and draw the symbol on your forehead, your chest, or the back of your hand (or all of the above).

3. As you mark yourself, say: "I am made of dust. And to dust I will return. But while I'm here I will live with intention. I will change what needs changing. I will become who I was meant to be. Today, I will begin to get back on track."

4. Pause. Breathe. Let it land.

Name:

1. Look back on what you have written and ask yourself: What would be the easiest thing for me to change right now? What would be a simple first step that I know I can take? Write it down.

2. Then come up with the second easiest step and write it down. You don't need forty, but gather a handful.

3. Say them aloud.

4. Then read this slowly: "This is where I begin again. I will use the ashes of my mistakes to chart a new path. I will not let more of my life slip away before I begin trying to get back on track."

Close:

1. Sit in silence for one more minute.

2. Take deep breaths.

3. Quiet your mind again.

4. Then bring this hopeful thought into the center of your mind: "You don't need to take the first step toward getting back on track. You just took it. You've already started."

Make It Yours

What changes did or could you make to the ritual to better suit your context or needs?

Reflect

What did the ashes help you release?

What emotions rose up as you faced those endings?

What beginnings feel possible now?

Four

Feeling Disconnected from the World

Origins of this Ritual

This ritual is quite possibly the one that has informed and expanded the lives of the most people in history—likely over ten billion. Traditionally, Communion commemorates the Last Supper of Jesus with his disciples. That meal was part of a larger Jewish festival called Passover, which focused on passing the story of the Exodus down to the next generation. In that story, the people of Israel are enslaved, and God sends a deliverer (Moses) to stand up against the powerful and lead the people out of bondage.

In the Last Supper, Jesus takes the unleavened bread—the bread of affliction—and says, "This is my body, broken for you." Then he takes the cup and says, "This is my blood of the new covenant, poured out for you and for many, for the forgiveness of sins. Do this often in remembrance of me." This ritual has united Christians together for millennia.

But there is a deeply mystical aspect of Communion. Christians don't just see this as uniting a church together in the moment they share it, but as uniting them with all Christians everywhere who have ever lived. The Communion table in a church is not just a table—it is connected to every table, including Christ's own table during that last supper.

This adaptation builds on that connection by using the traditional form of the communion ritual and its connection to food to process the mystical reality that all humans are, indeed, connected to all humans everywhere who have ever lived—and to all of creation itself through the food we eat. Because every human who dies eventually becomes part of the earth, their body is ultimately the ground from which the grass grows that feeds the livestock we consume, and the soil from which our vegetables, fruits, and nuts grow. When we think deeply, we realize there is no living thing to which we are not connected.

And that connection provides accountability. If we are connected to everything, our care for nature and for others is also care for ourselves. When we wound others or the earth, we are wounding ourselves. This deep connection calls us to live in ways that restore and nurture—not exploit or destroy—the shared body of life we all belong to.

Modern psychology offers a mirror to this ancient intuition. Studies in moral and social psychology show that shared meals foster empathy and reduce perceived difference. When we eat together, our brains release oxytocin—the same neurochemical linked to bonding and trust. The ritual of eating in sync with others activates what researchers call interpersonal synchrony, helping us feel more connected and less defensive. Communion, then, is more than metaphor—it's a neurological and emotional pattern that rewires us toward compassion.

As an echo of that connection, this ritual engages all of our senses. We hear the words spoken aloud, feel the food and drink as we consume and taste it, and smell the aroma as we bring it to our mouths. And we see the beauty of the food that connects us to everything and everyone on earth.

Ritual

Prepare:

1. Before you begin, gather something to eat and drink.

2. If possible, set a table for a nice meal. Have all the silverware for yourself and any of your guests.

3. You may choose to set that "table" on a blanket outside to be even more aware of your connection to nature.

4. This can be powerful by yourself or with others.

Centering:

1. Light the candle.

2. As the flame flickers into being, remember: rituals like this help us see more clearly. Even when the world feels dim or dark or uncertain, this light is here to help you find your way.

3. Speak aloud or in your heart: "All are welcome here. At this table, all belong. We are all dust. We are all earth. We are stardust—made of everything that ever was and everything that ever will be."

4. As you sit with this light and this truth, let your breath slow. Let your body settle into the space you've chosen. Let yourself arrive fully.

Coming clean:

1. We are all connected by what we eat. But we know what it feels like to be disconnected, too—to harm with our words or silence, to ignore the cries of others or the earth, to forget that we are held together in this shared life.

2. Take a moment to come clean, to confess where you have gotten off track. You can speak it aloud, write it down, or whisper it to the universe. Whatever it looks like, let this be a moment of honest reflection.

3. Say aloud or in your heart: "To the universe, to the earth, to those I've/we've harmed, to myself/ourselves—I/We come clean."

Remembering the table:

1. Every spiritual tradition has its own way of making food sacred—the Passover feast, the cake-and-ale rite, iftar at sundown, Communion, Holi, countless others.

2. Sitting together and eating is never just about calories. It's about connection—about seeing the divine in each other and in the soil that feeds us.

3. Say aloud or in your heart: "In this moment, I/we join that ancient thread. I/we add my/our voice(s) to that long song. I/we sit at a table that stretches across the world."

Blessing the meal:

1. Hold your food in your hands. Let it remind you that your body is made of earth, your flesh is holy, and your hands can be instruments of care. Eat.

2. Hold your drink. Let it remind you of the water that falls from the sky, the womb that held you, and the way life keeps pulsing through everything. Drink.

Committing to the connection:

1. As you swallow, say this aloud or in your heart—this is your commitment: "I/we will remember that I belong to this earth. I/we will remember that I belong to others. I/we will honor the sacredness of food, body, and breath. I/we will live like I am not alone. Because I/we am/are not. I/we belong."

2. Blow out the candle, but carry its light with you.

Make It Yours

What changes did or could you make to the ritual to better suit your context
or needs?

25

Reflect

What moments in the meal felt most grounding or sacred?

26

What stories or memories came alive as you ate?

How might you live differently in response to what you receive?

Five

LIVING IN A SPACE THAT HOLDS PAIN

Origins of this Ritual

This ritual draws inspiration from the smudging practices found in many Indigenous cultures—particularly among Native American and First Nations peoples—where sacred smoke is used for cleansing, healing, and protection. Traditionally, smudging involves the burning of specific herbs such as white sage, sweetgrass, cedar, or tobacco. The fragrant smoke is guided around a person, object, or space, often with a feather or hand, as part of a ceremony to clear away negative energy and invite balance, clarity, or blessing.

But smudging is far more than an aromatic ritual—it is a sacred act rooted in community, memory, land, and relationship. In many traditions, smudging is part of a broader ceremonial life: performed before prayer, healing, council meetings, or major life transitions. Some Indigenous people smudge daily as a way of grounding in spiritual presence, and the act is almost always accompanied by prayer or song. The plants themselves are considered sacred relatives, not simply tools.

This ritual does not attempt to replicate or borrow directly from any one tribal custom. Instead, it draws on the symbolic power of smoke itself—a universal and ancient element across cultures—to create a space for intentional release and re-inscription of memory. Fire transforms the material world; smoke carries what has been burned into the unseen. Across time and continents, people have used smoke to carry prayers, mark transitions, and clear spaces. This version joins that long human tradition while avoiding appropriation by using accessible, non-specific materials and by explicitly naming the intention: not to imitate, but to honor.

The goal here is not to manipulate energy, but to engage the body, senses, and imagination in a process of mental and emotional release—to let go of painful memories, stories, or associations that no longer serve you, and invite your brain to write a new narrative.

Contemporary psychological research confirms the impact of rituals like this. According to studies in trauma therapy and cognitive neuroscience, symbolic physical gestures—especially those involving movement, scent, and multi-sensory focus—can create real changes in the way memories are encoded and recalled. Burning or releasing a symbol tied to a painful memory allows the brain to reprocess the emotion, reduce its intensity, and create an embodied sense of closure. Smell in particular is deeply tied to memory through the olfactory bulb, which connects directly to the amygdala and hippocampus—centers of emotional memory and learning. This is why certain scents can trigger powerful memories—and why choosing a new scent during a release ritual can help the mind mark the beginning of a different association.

By using fragrant smoke, breath, and mindful attention, this ritual creates a moment in which you are not just remembering—you are rewriting. Letting old memories loosen their grip. Letting scent and motion offer something new. Letting go of what clings to the past so you can make room for the life ahead.

Prepare:

You'll need:

1. Sage, palo santo, incense, or another fragrant herb you connect with

2. A small fire-safe bowl or tray

3. Something to light it with

4. A window to open or a door to crack, so the old energy has somewhere to go

Pick a time when your space is quiet. Turn off your notifications. Put your phone face down. If you'd like, play instrumental music that helps you feel grounded or safe.

Ritual

Begin at the threshold:

1. Stand at the entrance of your home—or whatever space you want to cleanse. Light the herb or incense and let the smoke rise. Pause. Watch it curl and drift.

2. Take a deep breath and say: "This smoke carries away what no longer belongs here."

3. You can whisper it. You can think it. You can say it with your full voice.

Walk with intention:

1. Move slowly through the space, wafting the smoke with your hand or a feather if you like. Let your pace be steady but unhurried.

2. Spend extra time in places that hold difficult memories—your bedroom, a corner where you had a hard conversation, the doorway where the bad news came in.

3. As you move, read and internalize the statements, and then say out loud: "This sadness doesn't belong to me anymore." "I release the fear I carried in this room." "I let go of the story that kept repeating here." "This place is no longer stuck in that version of me."

4. Breathe in and out and let the smoke speak for you.

Invite what you need:

1. When you've made your way through the space, return to the place you began.

2. This time, go back through and speak aloud the kind of energy you want to welcome in.

3. As you move, read and internalize the statements, and then say out loud: "Let this room hold softness." "Let this kitchen feed joy." "Let this hallway echo with laughter." "Let this bed be a place of rest and tenderness."

4. Breathe in and out and let the smoke speak for you.

Seal the shift:

1. Stand again at the entrance. Let the smoke curl up one last time.

2. Envision and internalize all that you have let leave and all that you have asked to enter.

3. Say aloud: "Let the new begin."

4. Blow out the embers. Thank the smoke. Then open a window or the door, even just for a moment, and let the air move. Let the energy shift. Let the old exit and the new enter.

5. Then go back in.

Make It Yours

What changes did or could you make to the ritual to better suit your context or needs?

Reflect

How did the space feel before and after the ritual?

32

What energy or presence do you want to welcome in now?

What layers of emotional or spiritual residue were carried out with the smoke?

Six

Feeling Afraid of What's Ahead

Origins of this Ritual

This ritual draws inspiration from the Hindu tradition of lighting a Diya—a small clay or metal oil lamp—especially during Diwali, the Festival of Lights. Celebrated across South Asia and the global Hindu diaspora, Diwali commemorates the triumph of light over darkness, wisdom over ignorance, and justice over oppression. Families place Diyas in doorways, windows, and on household altars to welcome blessings into their homes and lives.

Traditionally, lighting a Diya is more than a decorative gesture. It is an act of reverence. The flame is seen as a representation of divine presence and the inner light that exists within each person. In many homes, lighting a Diya is accompanied by prayer, meditation, or offerings—serving as a spiritual anchor in daily life and a reminder of the sacred that lives in the ordinary.

This ritual adaptation honors the essence of that practice while shifting its focus inward. Here, you are not invoking a god or marking a festival. You are awakening the divine spark within yourself. The act of lighting a candle becomes an embodied commitment to carry that light forward—to enter your day with clarity, integrity, and compassion.

Psychologically, this practice is supported by findings in behavioral science and cognitive anchoring theory. Research shows that symbolic actions performed with intention—especially those involving light, flame, or motion—can influence how we frame our experience and perceive ourselves. Lighting a flame in a dark room can act as a visual cue that reorients our mind, triggering what psychologists call a "salience shift." In other words, by deliberately focusing on light, we train our awareness toward clarity, possibility, and resilience.

Even a small flame can change how we feel. In studies of ritualized behavior and emotional regulation, participants who performed a simple lighting or extinguishing ritual reported an increased sense of purpose and reduced anxiety compared to those who engaged in the same task without ritual framing. It's not the flame itself that changes us, but what we allow it to represent.

In this ritual, the candle becomes a mirror of your own inner presence. Lighting it is a declaration: "I am not passive in the face of darkness. I bring light with me."

Prepare:

You'll need:

1. A small candle, oil lamp, or tea light

2. A safe surface near where you get ready

3. A moment of quiet before the day begins

Set your alarm a few minutes earlier than usual. Try to keep your phone on silent. This doesn't have to take long, but give it your full attention.

Ritual

Start in darkness:

1. Begin your morning in dim or complete darkness. No overhead lights—just you, the stillness, and the shadow of what's to come.

2. Strike a match and light your candle.

3. As the flame catches, think first, then whisper: "From the darkness,

I rise. From the stillness, I shine."

4. Let the glow fill the room slowly. Let your eyes adjust. Let yourself notice how just one flame changes everything.

Welcome the flame:

1. As you move through your morning routine—washing your face, brushing your teeth, choosing your clothes—glance back at the candle.

2. Let it become a quiet companion, a reminder that you have warmth to give, that you have light others need, that even when the world feels dim, you carry fire.

3. When you notice the candle, say one of these phrases: "May this light move through me." "May I be a comfort to those in darkness." "May I bring clarity where there's confusion, hope where there's pain."

4. Or just breathe and watch the flame dance for a moment. Let it say what you can't yet put into words.

Send the light with you:

1. Right before you leave—when your keys are in your hand and the door is waiting—go back to the candle.

2. Pause. Let the moment stretch.

3. Blow it out slowly. Watch the smoke curl and disappear.

4. Then say: "The flame is not gone. I carry it in me now."

5. Step into the day lit from within.

Make It Yours

What changes did or could you make to the ritual to better suit your context or needs?

Reflect

What shifted in you as the flame began to glow?

How does carrying this light within you change how you face what's coming?

What does the flame teach you about your own strength when the path ahead feels uncertain?

Seven

Forgetting That You Already Have Enough

Origins of this Ritual

Everywhere humans have lived, we've turned to the earth with open hands. Long before organized religion, before temples or scriptures, people built small piles of stones. They left food at the base of trees. They whispered thanks to rivers and lit candles on the ground—not to get something in return, but because they knew something sacred was happening every time they reached down and picked up what the world had grown.

You can still see these rituals today. In Wiccan and neo-pagan circles, it's common to leave small offerings on an altar—a flower, a feather, a bit of fruit—as a sign of gratitude and connection to the elements. In ancient Celtic traditions, sacred wells and groves were places to leave small gifts in exchange for healing, blessing, or simply as a thank-you. And among Indigenous peoples around the world—from the Ojibwe offering tobacco to the earth before gathering plants, to the Māori burying placenta in the soil to connect newborns to the land—there's a deep, lasting sense that the earth gives, and we give back.

This ritual builds on that instinct. It doesn't ask you to perform someone else's practice. Instead, it gives you a framework to make your own and incorporate any spirituality underneath it you like, or not. The point isn't the object—it's the pause. The moment you realize that what's growing around you is still feeding you. Still sustaining you. Still offering you what you need.

And when you begin your day by noticing that? That's where the magic starts.

Psychologically, offering rituals tap into a deeply rooted neurological principle: attention shapes experience. When we take even a few seconds to give thanks for something tangible—a piece of fruit, a leaf, a smooth stone—we activate the brain's default mode network in a way that increases empathy, reduces anxiety, and fosters a sense of connection.

Research in positive psychology shows that micro-acts of gratitude—especially when they're physical, not just verbal—can reorient the brain's attention toward abundance rather than lack. These small rituals help interrupt the autopilot of modern life and remind us of our place in the broader web of life, not as consumers but as participants.

The result isn't just a better mood—it's a shift in how we see the world. We begin to approach the day not with entitlement or scarcity, but with humility and wonder. And that shift in posture has a ripple effect: it improves our relationships, decision-making, and ability to respond with care rather than reactivity.

Prepare:

You'll need:

1. A small plate, shallow bowl, or space to act as your altar (a windowsill works just fine)

2. A place to pause for a moment, even if it's just by the door or the kitchen sink

Over time, this collection becomes a kind of living altar—a record of your attention, a grounding in gratitude for the daily gifts the world offers.

Ritual

Step outside or face a window:

1. Before grabbing your phone, before the rush of what's next, step out or turn toward the natural world—even if it's just a crack of sky between buildings or the tree outside your apartment.

2. Take a breath. Let it stretch. Notice something around you that's growing, fallen, or free.

3. Let your eyes wander and find a small object that catches your attention. This isn't about what's pretty or impressive; it's about what pulls at you. Trust your gut.

4. Once you find the object, take it in your hand and return to a space where it can stay as a reminder and a consistent grounding.

Place the offering:

1. Take your object to your plate or altar space. Set it down like you're giving it a place of honor.

2. Say aloud or whisper: "The earth gives to me. May I seek the nourishment I need today."

3. Pause. Breathe. Let your body feel the weight of that truth.

4. Visualize that this object is holding the goodness the earth has already given you—the air you're breathing, the food you'll eat, the people who love you, and even the challenges that might help you grow.

Let it ground you:

1. Take one more breath and ask yourself: What kind of nourishment do I need today? Where do I feel depleted? What would it look like to let the earth give back to me?

2. You don't need an answer. Just asking is enough.

3. Then, move into whatever is next, leaving the offering behind to

ground you again.

Some days this will feel sacred. Other days it won't. That's okay. Rituals like this aren't magic tricks. They're daily choices to notice—and when you notice the earth giving to you, even in small, quiet ways, it's easier to move through the day with gratitude, with your feet on the ground, and with a heart open to receive.

Make It Yours

What changes did or could you make to the ritual to better suit your context or needs?

Reflect

What changed as you paused to receive rather than grasp?

Where in your life did you feel more connected after this moment of giving back?

What have you already been given that you haven't fully acknowledged yet?

Eight

Missing Someone Who's Gone

Origins of this Ritual

Sometimes the best way to remember someone isn't a gravestone or a eulogy—it's a casserole. A spice that hits just right. A dessert that tastes like childhood. And the telling of stories about the people we've loved and lost.

This ritual draws from Día de los Muertos (Day of the Dead), a vibrant tradition that began with the Aztecs and evolved into a beautiful fusion of Indigenous spirituality and Catholic practice. Originally, it was a month-long festival honoring Mictecacihuatl, the Lady of the Dead. Later, it merged with All Saints' and All Souls' Days to become the colorful, food-filled celebration many know today.

But what makes it powerful isn't the decorations or the customs—it's the insistence that the dead are not gone. They live on when we remember them. When we light candles, speak their names, set out the things they loved, and tell their stories out loud. That act of remembering isn't nostalgia—it's connection.

In traditional Día de los Muertos celebrations, families build ofrendas (altars) at home or in cemeteries, adorned with marigolds—bright orange flowers believed to guide spirits with their vivid color and strong scent—and sugar skulls that celebrate the beauty and impermanence of life. And at the center of each ofrenda are the photos and artifacts of the ones we miss.

This version of the ritual draws from that deep well of wisdom while making space for anyone—religious or not—to participate in the sacred act of remembering. Here, the meal becomes the altar. The stories become the offering. And the presence of those we miss becomes real again through memory.

Modern psychology affirms what this ancient practice teaches: our memories are not static—they are relational and embodied. Telling stories aloud, especially while engaged in a shared physical act like cooking or eating, strengthens our emotional connection to the person we've lost. Neurologically, this activates parts of the brain associated with attachment and identity, helping us metabolize grief not by suppressing it, but by integrating it into our ongoing lives.

When we gather around a table, taste the food they loved, and speak their name, we're not just remembering—we're reconnecting. And that has the power to soften sorrow, rekindle joy, and anchor us more fully in the present.

Grief doesn't go away. But when we eat together, remember together, and carry their stories forward—we don't carry them alone. Not in silence. But around a table.

Prepare:

Before the ritual:

1. Invite friends or family to bring food that reminds them of someone who has died. This could be a dish that person used to cook, a snack they always kept around, or something that sparks a memory or inside joke.

2. Ask participants to bring a photo of the person they're remembering. They can also bring a memento or the person's written name.

3. Create an ofrenda—a small table or area where those photos and objects can be placed together, surrounded by candles, skulls, or flowers if you have them. It is wonderful if the food can also be on this table.

4. Choose a space where everyone can eat, speak, and be present with each other.

You'll need:

1. A candle for each person being remembered

2. Optional: background music the remembered people loved, flowers (especially marigolds), or incense

Ritual

Gathering the table:

1. As people arrive, invite them to place their photos and mementos on the ofrenda and, if there is space, their dish.

2. Before sitting down to eat, stand around the ofrenda together. Let each person take a moment to show the photo they brought and say the name of the person they're remembering. Let them tell what the food is that they brought, and also let them know you will share stories later.

3. Then, light the candle and say: "This table is set with memory and love. We light this flame to welcome those who are no longer here, but who remain alive in the stories we carry and the food we share."

Sharing the memories:

1. As you eat, invite stories—big or small. This isn't a eulogy. It's a table of life. As you introduce this time, help people's imaginations and memories spark by offering these questions: What's something they used to say all the time? How did they show you love? What's a moment that still makes you laugh? Is there a smell, sound, or food that brings them back? What's something quirky or surprising about them?

2. Remind everyone that this doesn't need to be somber. It doesn't need to be profound. If it mattered to you, it matters here.

3. Ask each person to light a candle before they talk about each person they are remembering and then tell a story.

4. Let silence come when it needs to. Let tears or laughter show up without explanation.

Closing the circle:

1. When the meal ends, return focus to the ofrenda. Stand or sit together in silence for a few breaths.

2. Then say aloud: "We are made of stories. And when we tell them, we keep the people we love alive. May their stories live on in us."

3. Blow out the candles together.

4. You may choose to leave the ofrenda up for a few more days or take a photo of it before putting things away as a keepsake. Some people relight the candle the next night as a continuation of the remembrance.

Make It Yours

What changes did or could you make to the ritual to better suit your context or needs?

Reflect

What memories felt especially alive in this ritual?

50

What was it like to make space for their presence again?

How might their stories continue in your life now?

Nine

TRYING TO CHANGE A PATTERN THAT'S STUCK

Origins of this Ritual

This ritual draws inspiration from ancient mourning and transformation practices found throughout the Hebrew Bible and many other spiritual traditions. One of the most visceral of these involved wearing sackcloth—a coarse, scratchy material often made from goat or camel hair. In biblical times, donning sackcloth was a public signal of mourning, remorse, or deep personal change. It was not subtle. The discomfort was the point. Each itch and scrape against the skin served as a physical reminder that something inside needed reckoning.

In this reimagined ritual, the gesture becomes quieter but no less meaningful. Instead of a full sackcloth garment worn for all to see, you carry a small piece of rough fabric discreetly—maybe tucked into a pocket, wrapped around a wrist, or pinned inside your clothing. It's not meant to draw attention; it's meant to call your attention back to what you're trying to shift. The texture against your skin becomes a kind of somatic whisper—a silent, tactile reminder of the change you're inviting.

This practice draws on a profound psychological truth: transformation doesn't happen in the abstract. It happens in the body.

Modern neuroscience shows us that our habits, beliefs, and patterns are wired not just in our thoughts but in our nervous system. When we move through the world unconsciously, our brains default to well-worn neural paths—many of them formed years ago in moments of survival, shame, or pain. True transformation often begins with interrupting those paths. And sometimes, the body can help do that.

Wearing something mildly uncomfortable as a cue is not new to psychology. From rubber bands used in behavior-change therapy to tactile fidgets that ground anxious minds, we know that minor physical disruptions can make room for new awareness. That's what this ritual taps into. When your attention drifts, when old patterns creep back in, that tiny pull of fabric brings you back. You remember: This is what I'm changing.

Ritual

Choose your reminder:

1. Find a small piece of fabric that's mildly uncomfortable to wear—something like burlap, raw linen, or unfinished canvas. The goal isn't pain, just a gentle but noticeable texture that catches your attention throughout the day. If you have sensory sensitivity, choose something like a bracelet or other item to wear.

2. You might: Cut a square of fabric and pin it inside your sleeve. Tie a thin strip around your wrist or ankle. Sew it inside the waistband of your clothes. Place it in an undergarment.

3. Before putting it on, name the change you're hoping to make. Speak it aloud or write it down: "I am releasing..." or "I am becoming..."

Wear it with intention:

1. Set a time frame—an hour, a day, or a full week. As you go about your routine, let the sensation of the fabric call your attention back.

2. When you notice discomfort, pause for a couple of seconds. Inhale slowly. On the exhale, say, "I stay awake to my own transformation." Then repeat your change statement: "I am releasing..." or "I am becoming..."

3. If you have more time in the moment, ask: "Why am I doing this?" "What am I letting go of?" "What am I choosing instead?"

4. You can pair this with a breath practice if you wish.

Remove it with ceremony:

1. When your chosen period ends, don't just toss the fabric aside. Let it be a moment of closure.

2. Take a few breaths while holding the fabric in your hand. Whisper to the fabric, "I am thankful for the focus and reminder you have brought."

3. Burn the cloth or bury it, imagining the thing you were trying to change leaving your life.

4. Say aloud or silently: "I honor the change I have begun."

Make It Yours

What changes did or could you make to the ritual to better suit your context or needs?

Reflect

What resistance surfaced while practicing?

What habits or beliefs began to feel more visible?

What small steps might begin to shift those patterns?

Ten

BEFORE THE HARD CONVERSATION

Origins of this Ritual

This ritual draws inspiration from the Jewish tradition of Tashlich, practiced during the High Holy Days. In Tashlich, participants symbolically cast their sins into flowing water—often by throwing crumbs, pebbles, or bread—while also shaking out the corners of their garments or emptying their pockets to represent the shedding of moral or spiritual burdens. It is a tactile, embodied act of letting go.

In this adapted version, the same symbolism is used as a preparation for difficult conversations. Whether it's resentment, fear, or unspoken expectations, we often carry invisible baggage into conflict—baggage that makes it harder to listen, connect, or repair.

Psychologists affirm that naming and releasing these emotional weights ahead of time helps us respond more thoughtfully rather than react defensively. Journaling about what we need to let go of activates the prefrontal cortex, reducing emotional reactivity. And physical gestures—like emptying our pockets—create muscle memory for new ways of showing up.

This ritual joins ancient spiritual wisdom with modern psychological insight: before we speak, we empty. Before we confront, we unburden.

Prepare:

You'll need:

1. A small piece of paper and a pen or pencil

2. A quiet space where you can reflect undisturbed for a few minutes

3. A trash bin or other way to dispose of paper

Ritual

Ground yourself:

1. Find a few minutes to be still. Sit down, close your eyes if it helps, and take three slow, deep breaths. Let your mind settle—not perfectly, just enough.

2. Ask yourself three questions: What am I bringing into this conversation? What hurts, fears, or expectations might be shaping the story I'm telling myself? What might I need to lay down in order to truly listen?

Name what you're carrying:

1. Write down anything that might keep you from being present: Resentment or frustration. The need to be right. Fear of being misunderstood. Expectations for how the conversation "should" go.

2. If words are hard to find, try this phrase: "I'm letting go of..."and then list whatever comes up.

Release it:

1. Read what you wrote, taking a breath after each item.

2. Slowly and with intention, destroy or discard the paper—tear it up, crumple it, or drop it in the trash.

3. As you destroy the paper, say: "I release this. I choose to show up open."

4. Stand up. Then turn your pockets inside out. Let the fabric hang.

5. As you do, say: "I empty what clings to me. Let me carry only what's needed."

6. Sit down, close your eyes if it helps, and take three slow, deep breaths.

Enter the conversation with intention:

1. Before you step into the conversation, pause one more time and say: "I enter this with curiosity, not certainty. I bring my honesty and my care."

2. Then walk in—just a little more spacious, a little more free.

Make it Yours

What changes did or could you make to the ritual to better suit your context or needs?

Reflect

What became clearer once you grounded yourself?

Which values feel most important to carry into conversations like this?

What fears or stories felt smaller after the ritual?

Eleven

STRUGGLING WITH THE HARM YOU'VE CAUSED

Origins of this Ritual

This ritual draws from the ancient scapegoat ceremony described in the Hebrew Bible (Leviticus 16), part of the Jewish tradition of Yom Kippur, the Day of Atonement. In that ceremony, a goat was symbolically burdened with the people's collective wrongs and sent into the wilderness—carrying their moral failings far away from the community.

A vivid detail from later rabbinic tradition added a striking symbol: a scarlet thread tied around the goat's horns or around the temple gates. This red thread was said to turn white when the people's repentance was accepted—a poetic image of transformation. But even without the miracle, the thread served as a reminder: here is what we carry, here is what we hope to release.

In this modern version, we keep the essence of the ritual: the embodied release of regret, accountability, and the choice to begin again. But we shift the focus from individual guilt to the harm we've caused in others and in the world—intentionally or not. The aim is not shame or punishment, but responsibility and reconnection.

This ritual is supported by psychological insights: research shows that naming and externalizing guilt, especially through physical actions like throwing or tying, can reduce shame, increase empathy, and help people move toward repair. Symbolic release helps us process our mistakes and return to the world with humility and clarity.

Prepare:

You'll need:

1. Access to moving water—a stream, river, ocean tide, or even a fountain

2. Two small natural objects with some weight, like stones or twigs

3. A short piece of red thread, yarn, or string, or a piece of red cloth like a bandana, large enough to tie

4. A moment of quiet, alone or with others

Ritual

Tie the thread:

1. Hold one of your objects and your piece of red thread or red fabric.

2. As you tie the thread around the object, name aloud or in your heart the harm you carry: "For the times I've spoken in anger or silence when someone needed me." "For the damage I've done, knowingly or not." "For when I've fallen short of who I want to be." "For the impact I've had when I wasn't paying attention."

3. Let the thread and the object absorb that weight. Feel it—not to punish yourself, but to name what's real.

4. Say: "This is the harm I've caused. I face it honestly." "I carry this now with full awareness."

5. Remove the thread or fabric from the object and tie it around your wrist or finger.

Approach the water:

1. Step slowly toward the water. Let its presence soften you.

2. When you're ready, hold the object tightly in your hand. Pay

attention to how its surface feels. This is the burden you are releasing—not forgetting, but letting go of the weight so you can move forward.

3. Say: "I acknowledge the pain I've caused." "I release the harm I cannot undo." "May this flow from me like water."

4. Toss the object into the current. Watch it go. Let the sight of the item in or on the water hold what you no longer need to carry.

Begin again with intention:

1. Take your second object—this one symbolizing your intention to live differently, to repair what you can, to remain committed to growth.

2. Hold it close to your chest and feel the new intention.

3. Release it gently into the water.

4. Say: "I begin again." "I return to what matters."

5. Untie the thread from your wrist, or keep it on as a quiet reminder of your intention for the next day, week, or season.

Make It Yours

What changes did or could you make to the ritual to better suit your context or needs?

Reflect

What truth felt hardest to name as you tied the thread?

67

How did it feel to let the water carry what you could no longer hold?

What intention do you want the red thread to remind you of as you move forward?

Twelve

NEEDING WISDOM YOU CAN'T FIND ALONE

Origin of this Ritual

Across cultures and centuries, people have looked to the stars not just for beauty or navigation, but for connection—to something older, wiser, and beyond the self. Many Indigenous traditions understand ancestors as part of the ongoing fabric of the universe, present in sky, land, wind, and water. In African cosmologies, ancestors are living presences who walk beside us. In Chinese and Japanese traditions, seasonal festivals honor the dead by lighting lanterns to guide their spirits. Ancient Egyptians associated stars with eternal life, believing the souls of the departed joined the constellations.

This ritual draws from that legacy of ancestral reverence and cosmic reflection. And it's more than spiritual: research shows that experiences of awe—like gazing into a vast starry sky—can reduce anxiety, increase humility, and improve our capacity for empathy and reflection. Psychology also reminds us that memory, imagination, and problem-solving often spring not from our conscious logic, but from our subconscious—the realm of dreams, intuition, and emotion.

When we bring questions to our ancestors—even in silence—we create a bridge to the deeper parts of ourselves. Letting their memory "speak" opens the door to insights we might otherwise miss. Their stories loosen our grip on the way we always think, and invite something new to surface. This is less about hearing words and more about sensing truth.

Prepare:

You'll need:

1. A somewhat clear night and a safe place to lie down

2. A journal or phone for voice notes (optional)

Don't worry if you can't see many stars. Even one will do. And if you're indoors, consider using a star projector, a sky simulation app, or simply a dark room with a candle.

Ritual

Prepare the space:

1. Choose a quiet spot where you can lie on your back and look upward.

2. Take a deep breath.

3. Say aloud or silently: "I come to listen." "I open myself to those who came before me."

Name your ancestor:

1. Think of an ancestor—by blood, adoption, or spirit—who shaped you. Someone whose memory, or your knowledge of their life, holds weight.

2. Say their name aloud. If no one comes to mind, you might simply say: "To the ones whose blood and stories I carry. I remember you."

3. Place a hand on your chest or belly as you breathe their presence into awareness.

Ask and imagine:

1. Form a question you want to ask. It might be about a decision, a fear, a relationship, or a change you're trying to make.

2. Ask aloud or silently: "What would you want me to know right now?" "How did you find courage when things were hard?" "What part of you is alive in me today?"

3. Then be still. Let the sky, your memory, and your imagination work together.You might hear their voice in your mind. You might see an image. You might just feel a shift inside. This is your subconscious opening space for wisdom. Trust what comes—or the silence that holds you.

Listen and receive:

1. Stay present under the stars for at least 5–10 minutes.

2. Don't force answers. Simply notice. What thoughts arise? What sensations come? What emotions stir?

3. If an insight comes, whisper "thank you," and write it down or record a voice note.

4. If nothing comes, whisper "I'm still listening."

Close in gratitude:

1. When you're ready to return, place your hand on the ground. Feel the connection between earth and sky, body and memory.

2. Stand up and look back at the sky.

3. Say: "I am held by those who came before me." "Their wisdom lives on in me."

4. If you brought a journal, jot down any reflections. If not, carry the moment with you into the days ahead.

Make It Yours

What changes did or could you make to the ritual to better suit your context or needs?

Reflect

What messages or images stayed with you afterward?

73

How did the silence feel different this time?

What do you sense this wisdom is asking of you now?

Thirteen

Not Knowing What You Believe Anymore

Origin of this Ritual

This ritual is inspired by Dhikr (Arabic: "remembrance"), a central spiritual practice in many Sufi and Islamic traditions. In Dhikr, practitioners repeat the names or attributes of God aloud or silently—sometimes hundreds of times—as a way of remembering, invoking, and embodying the presence of the divine. These names (like Al-Rahman, The Merciful, or Al-Haqq, The Truth) are drawn from the Qur'an and centuries of tradition. Over time, this meditative repetition becomes more than worship—it becomes intimacy.

But the practice of naming the Divine isn't limited to Islam. Across religions, spiritual seekers have used names—prayers, chants, mantras, and titles—to reach for something larger, more mysterious, and more loving than themselves. Names help shape our relationship with the sacred. They give form to what's hard to describe.

This ritual adapts that ancient impulse to remember and name, but makes space for those who are uncertain, skeptical, or disconnected from inherited images of God. You don't have to believe in a specific version of the Divine. You just have to wonder: "If God were real, who would I want them to be?"

From a psychological perspective, this can be a profound act of values clarification and projection. Naming what you long for in the Divine—justice, tenderness, strength, compassion—can help you identify what matters most to you. And in naming those traits repeatedly, you begin to awaken them within yourself.

This is a ritual of imagining the sacred and becoming it.

Prepare:

You'll need:

1. A quiet space

2. Pen and paper (or a phone note app)

3. 10–15 minutes of undistracted time

Ritual

Settle and reflect:

1. Find a quiet place. Sit or lie down comfortably.

2. Take three deep breaths. As you breathe, release any pressure to "do this right." This is about honesty, not perfection.

3. Ask yourself: What do I wish God was like? (Listen for 2 minutes) Take a deep breath. What qualities would I want the sacred to have? (Listen for 2 minutes)Take a deep breath. What do I need from something bigger than me? (Listen for 2 minutes)Take a deep breath. Let your answers come from emotion, memory, longing—even pain. Let your inner child speak.

Create your list:

1. Take your paper or phone and begin to write down words or phrases that describe the Divine you long for.

2. Keep going until it feels complete. Two is enough. Thirty is beautiful. There's no wrong number.

Read the names aloud:

1. When your list is ready, take a deep breath and begin reading each

word or phrase that describes the divine aloud three times.

2. Read slowly.

3. Notice the physical sensations of speaking them in your body. Feel the vibration your voice creates in your body.

4. As you notice those sensations, imagine it entering your breath, your bones, your being. Notice that the sound of your voice is coming from inside your body. This is prayer without dogma. This is naming what is holy in your hunger.

Close the space:

1. When you finish, pause in silence.

2. Say: "I carry these names within me." "These qualities are what I seek—and what I offer."

3. Fold the list and carry it with you.

4. Return to it when you forget who you are, or what you believe in.

5. Let the names remind you again.

Make It Yours

What changes did or could you make to the ritual to better suit your context or needs?

Reflect

Which qualities surprised you most as they appeared in your list?

What do these names reveal about your deepest hopes or wounds?

Which names felt most alive when you said them aloud?

Fourteen

Regrouping at the Door

Origin of this Ritual

This ritual is inspired by the ancient Jewish tradition of the mezuzah, a small scroll affixed to the doorframe of a home. Inside is a handwritten verse from the Torah: "You shall write them on the doorposts of your house and on your gates" (Deuteronomy 6:9). Observant Jews touch the mezuzah as they enter or leave, sometimes whispering a prayer. It's not superstition; it's orientation. A quiet act of remembering: here's what I believe, here's how I want to live.

Across time and culture, thresholds have held sacred meaning. In many Indigenous communities, entering a home involves a spoken blessing or the removal of shoes—not just for cleanliness, but for reverence. In Tibetan Buddhism, monks step over temple thresholds mindfully, pausing to shift intention. Even in everyday homes around the world, people whisper a wish as they cross the threshold (whether aloud or silently): let this space be peaceful, let what's next be kind.

We cross dozens of thresholds each day. But what if even one of them could help us remember?

Psychologically, this moment is powerful. Cognitive scientists have observed what's called the "doorway effect," a tendency for people to forget what they were doing or intending as soon as they walk into a new room. That's not just a distraction; it's design. Our minds use thresholds to segment events, shifting attention from one context to another. The brain says: new space, new focus.

But what if you decided what that new focus would be?

That's what this ritual does. It gives the threshold a voice—not to command or control you, but to remind you. You write your own words, your own hope, your own centering phrase. Then you place them where your brain is already preparing for change.

This is a ritual about choosing how you enter—so the next space meets you with clarity, not chaos.

Prepare:

You'll need:

1. A small piece of paper

2. A pen or pencil

3. Tape, or access to a rug, doormat, or floorboard near a doorway you pass often

This threshold becomes more than a doorway. It becomes a reminder: every time you pass through, you carry something sacred.

Ritual

1. Find a doorway that matters to you. It could be your front door, your bedroom, or your studio—somewhere you cross often.

2. Pause at the threshold. Take a breath. Let your body settle. Ask yourself: what truth do I want to carry with me every time I step through this door? Wait for the phrase to come. It might be a word, a sentence, a vow, or a hope.

3. Write it on the small piece of paper. Fold it if needed and roll it gently into a scroll. As you roll, say aloud or in your heart: "This I carry into what's next." "This I remember every time I pass through."

4. Place the scroll where it will remain close to the threshold—taped to

the inside of the doorframe, tucked under a mat, or placed on a shelf beside the entrance. You don't need to see it every day. You just need to know it's there.

5. Each time you cross that threshold, pause—even for half a second. Touch the frame. Feel the floor under your feet. Let your body remember the phrase you wrote in the scroll.

6. If the phrase no longer fits, create a new scroll. Thresholds change, and so do we.

Make It Yours

What changes did or could you make to the ritual to better suit your context or needs?

Reflect

What kind of energy or intention do you want to carry into the spaces you enter most often?

What did you notice about yourself when you paused before crossing the line between one space and another?

How might your life feel different if every doorway became a moment of remembering?

Fifteen

Carrying Something for Someone Else

Origin of this Ritual

This ritual draws from the practice of intercessory prayer found in many religious traditions—where people offer prayers on behalf of others who are suffering, struggling, or in need. In Christianity, this often takes the form of lifting someone's name in prayer during worship or holding their image in mind during personal devotion. In Buddhism, Metta meditation involves sending loving-kindness toward others, especially those who are hurting. Across Indigenous traditions, shamans, elders, and community members have carried the emotional and spiritual burdens of others in ceremony, acting as mediators or compassionate witnesses for the healing process.

At the heart of these practices is one idea: you can hold space for someone else when they can't hold it for themselves. You don't have to speak for them or fix anything. You just have to stay with their pain—not turn away from it.

This ritual brings that tradition into physical form. It's not about saving or rescuing. It's about empathy that lives in your body. By choosing an object to carry, you make their burden tangible. You move through your day not just thinking of them, but holding them close, letting your concern take shape as presence.

Psychologically, this kind of symbolic action can deepen emotional attunement. Research on empathic resonance shows that people who take on small, voluntary burdens in solidarity with others report higher levels of connectedness and purpose. It also allows the mind to shift from helplessness to intention. You're not just worrying—you're witnessing, honoring, and staying close.

You may not be able to take away their pain. But by carrying something of theirs in your pocket, you remind yourself that love stays near even when there's nothing you can do, even when the weight is invisible.

Prepare:

You'll need:

1. A small object that fits in your pocket. Choose something with a bit of weight—like a stone, a metal token, a pendant, or a key.

Ritual

1. Hold the object in your hand and take a moment to center yourself.

2. Bring to mind the person whose pain, struggle, or situation you're holding. This might be a friend in crisis, a family member you're worried about, or someone who doesn't know you're holding them in your heart at all.

3. Name them silently or aloud. Let their presence come fully into your awareness.

4. Say: "I carry this, for now, with love."

5. Still holding the object, let the weight of their burden settle into it. You're not claiming it. You're witnessing it. Take a moment to remember that this isn't about fixing or saving—it's about choosing to stay connected, even when it hurts.

6. Say: "I can't take it away. But I will carry some of it with you today."

7. Place the object in your pocket. (If you don't have pockets, carry it in a bag, wear it, or keep it close. What matters is your intention.)As you go about your day, notice the object whenever you shift or

reach into your pocket. Let it ground you. Let it tether you back to compassion.

8. If a sense of frustration or helplessness rises, touch the object again. "I choose love over despair." "I will carry this as long as I need to."

9. At the end of the day, return to your quiet space. Hold the object one more time. Picture the person in your mind again. "This isn't mine to fix. But I haven't forgotten. "Place the object somewhere intentional—a nightstand, windowsill, or altar. Let it rest, and let yourself rest too.

Make It Yours

What changes did or could you make to the ritual to better suit your context or needs?

Reflect

How did holding this physical object change your awareness of the person you carried it for?

What emotions surfaced as you moved through your day with them in mind?

What do you want them to know—even if they never hear it?

Sixteen

STAYING GROUNDED IN WHO YOU ARE ALL DAY

Origin of this Ritual

This ritual is rooted in ancient practices of sacred body marking—an impulse found across time and culture. In Hindu and Muslim traditions, women decorate their hands with henna before significant life events as a form of spiritual protection and celebration. In Jewish tradition, some mourners pin a torn ribbon to their clothes (keriah) as an external symbol of internal grief. Christian pilgrims in the Middle Ages often tattooed small crosses on their forearms as a mark of devotion. Across African, Indigenous American, and Polynesian cultures, symbolic tattoos have long expressed identity, lineage, and spiritual connection.

Within mystical and magical traditions, writing directly on the body also carries intention. In chaos magic and other modern occult practices, sigils—symbols crafted to represent a specific goal or desire—are drawn on skin to serve as a focus for energy and transformation. These marks aren't just decoration. They're reminders. Anchors. Tools for embodiment.

Psychology echoes this wisdom. Studies in symbolic cognition suggest that symbols associated with emotions or values are often more vivid and easier to recall than written language. Research from the University of Waterloo (2023) showed that participants retained and emotionally responded to images more deeply than to equivalent words. Meanwhile, work on condensation symbols—used in rhetoric and branding—demonstrates how simple images can carry complex meaning and provoke strong personal associations.

Other studies on encoded cognition and body-focused reminders show that wearing or displaying personally meaningful symbols can influence attention, decision-making, and even mood throughout the day. When a message is written on your skin, your mind treats it differently. It's not just a note—it becomes a part of you.

This ritual channels all of that: the ancestral urge to mark the body with sacred intention, the spiritual impulse to carry something holy throughout the day, and the psychological truth that symbols can shift your focus in powerful ways.

It begins with a word or a symbol. A name you want to remember. A trait you want to live into. A truth you don't want to forget. You draw it on your skin—not for others to see, but so you can carry it with you. Quietly. Confidently.

Prepare:

You'll need:

1. A non-toxic, skin-safe marker or makeup pencil (something that will wash off easily)

2. Optional: a mirror

Ritual

1. Find a quiet moment and settle yourself in a relaxed posture.

2. Take a few deep breaths and ask: What part of me is most at risk of getting lost today? What truth about myself do I want to carry with me throughout the day? Sit with the question. Let the answer surface—not what sounds impressive, but what feels essential. A word. A phrase. A symbol.

3. Choose a spot on your body that you'll notice throughout the day; it may be visible to others or only visible to you in specific moments. Draw or write the word, phrase, or symbol slowly. As you do, say

(aloud or silently):"This is what I choose to remember." "This is who I am." Pause. Look at the mark. Let its presence settle deep in your mind.

4. Go about your day with the mark on your body. Let it speak to you when you glance at it. If you begin to feel like you are losing yourself (or have lost yourself), take a moment to look at the mark.

5. At the end of the day, when you see the mark still faintly on your skin—or after it's rubbed off completely—pause again. You can wash it away now. Or draw it again tomorrow. You're allowed to come back to yourself as many times as it takes.

Make It Yours

What changes did or could you make to the ritual to better suit your context or needs?

Reflect

What feeling or memory was connected to the word or symbol you chose?

How did carrying this message on your skin affect the way you related to others—or to yourself?

What will you choose to remember next time?

Meditation Practices

Seventeen

Entering Through the Image

Origin

This practice, known for centuries in the Eastern Orthodox tradition as icon gazing, began as a way of seeing beyond the surface of painted wood and pigment. In Byzantine spirituality, icons were not meant to be admired as art—they were windows to heaven, tangible portals through which unseen realities could be encountered. The word icon comes from the Greek *eikōn*, meaning "image" or "likeness." To gaze upon an icon was to meet a presence, not to look at a picture.

The practice grew from the conviction that the sacred can be encountered through the material. In Orthodox theology, the Incarnation—the belief that the divine took on flesh—made such a way of seeing possible: if the holy could dwell in a body, then even wood and paint could become vessels of encounter. For early monks, gazing at an icon was not about study or analysis but about letting their attention soften until something deeper emerged—until the eyes rested and the heart began to perceive.

Over time, this practice became a universal form of contemplative seeing. It is not confined to a particular faith. To gaze steadily upon a sacred image, or any image created with reverence, is to enter into relationship with it—to quiet the mind's analysis and allow the act of seeing itself to become prayer. When sustained, this kind of looking begins to feel mutual, as though the image itself were gazing back. Whether understood as divine reciprocity or as a profound psychological response to attention, the effect is the same: the image begins to shape the one who beholds it.

Psychologists describe this as reciprocal gaze, a phenomenon in which sustained visual attention activates the brain's mirror neuron systems and heightens emotional attunement. Prolonged looking reduces self-referential thought and strengthens empathy, creating what researchers call "shared presence." In contemplative contexts, this deepens into calm awareness and quiet resonance. Whether interpreted as communion with the sacred or alignment with inner stillness, entering through the image cultivates reciprocity between what is seen and the one who sees.

How to Practice

Choose the image:

Select an icon or sacred image that draws you—perhaps of Christ, Mary, a saint, or a figure of compassion or wisdom. It need not belong to any particular faith; what matters is that it carries a sense of reverence. Place it before you at eye level where you can see it easily and without strain.

Settle the body and breathe:

Sit comfortably with your back upright and your body relaxed. Take several slow, deep breaths—in through the nose, out through the mouth. Feel your body's weight supported and your breath steadying your awareness. Let your eyes soften and your attention grow still.

Rest the gaze:

Look at the image with gentle attention. Don't analyze or evaluate what you see. Simply rest your gaze, noticing color, form, and expression. If the eyes of the figure are visible, allow your gaze to meet theirs without strain or expectation.

Allow the encounter:

As you continue to gaze, notice what arises—thoughts, emotions, or subtle sensations. When distractions appear, acknowledge them and return softly to the image. Allow the image to draw you inward, as though you are being gently pulled into it. Let yourself move beyond its surface, entering through it into a deeper awareness. The goal is not to control the mind but to let perception open and widen.

Move into stillness:

When you feel ready, close your eyes while keeping the image in your awareness. Notice what remains—the impression, the warmth, or the quiet. Breathe slowly and rest in that inner space where seeing becomes being.

Conclude the practice:

Open your eyes. Take one final breath before continuing your day, carrying a trace of that stillness and quiet reciprocity with you.

Eighteen

Candle and Flame

Origin

This practice has ancient roots across cultures. In Christian monasteries, Hindu temples, and Buddhist shrines alike, a single flame has long symbolized the meeting of the visible and invisible. In early Christian mysticism, monks often described the candle as a reflection of the divine light within—the soul illuminated by attention. To gaze at a flame was to learn constancy from something that never ceases moving.

The flame exists only in the present. It cannot be held or captured; it renews itself moment by moment. Watching it teaches what language cannot: stillness within motion, presence within change. For those who sought the holy, this living light became a teacher of awareness—a reminder that the divine, or the deepest self, is found not in control but in continual becoming.

As the wax melts, it takes on a deeper symbolism of offering. The candle gives itself away to sustain its light. Monks and mystics saw in this the shape of devotion: transformation through surrender, warmth born from letting go. In more psychological terms, this act mirrors what contemplative practice accomplishes in the mind—the melting of rigid thought patterns into fluid presence.

Modern research supports what mystics intuited. Psychologists describe focused gazing at a flame as a form of trataka meditation, shown to calm the autonomic nervous system and quiet activity in the brain's default mode network, which drives rumination. The rhythmic dance of the flame synchronizes breathing and heart rate, reducing anxiety and enhancing sustained attention. The result is both ancient and scientific: a nervous system that mirrors the steady flicker of the flame—alive, calm, and awake.

How to Practice

Prepare the space:

Find a quiet room where you won't be disturbed. Place a candle at eye level, about an arm's length away. Dim other lights so the flame becomes the center of your vision.

Settle the body and breathe:

Sit comfortably with your back upright but relaxed. Take several slow, deep breaths—in through the nose, out through the mouth. Let your body grow still, your shoulders soften, and your breathing find a natural rhythm.

Gaze with soft eyes:

Look at the flame with gentle attention. Notice its color, shape, and movement. Don't force focus; simply observe. Allow the eyes to rest, following the rhythm of the flicker without strain. Notice how even in motion, the flame has a steady heart.

Breathe with the flame:

As you inhale, imagine drawing light into yourself. As you exhale, release gratitude or tension. Let your breath and the flame move together—each a reminder of the other's constancy.

Enter the silence:

When you're ready, close your eyes. You may see the flame's afterimage lingering behind your eyelids. Rest with it. Breathe softly and let the light fade into stillness, holding the quiet warmth it leaves behind.

Conclude the practice:

Open your eyes slowly. Take one final deep breath and notice the calm in your body. Extinguish the candle, carrying its steady glow inward as you return to your day.

Nineteen

Breath of the Body

Origin

Across traditions, breath has always carried sacred meaning. In Hebrew, the word *ruach* means both "breath" and "spirit." In Greek, *pneuma* carries the same double sense—wind, breath, life force. The ancient world knew what modern people easily forget: that each breath is both physical and spiritual, the invisible current that animates and connects all living things.

Mystics and contemplatives saw the body not as an obstacle to transcendence but as the very site of revelation. To become aware of one's own breathing was to remember what had been forgotten—that the sacred is not elsewhere, but within the rhythm of the body itself. Breath became prayer. Stillness became sanctuary.

In the early monastic movements of the desert, breath awareness was paired with posture and silence to train attention. Over centuries, this evolved into countless traditions of embodied prayer and meditation. Each teaches the same paradox: that to find stillness of spirit, one must first come home to the body.

Modern psychology now affirms what contemplatives long knew intuitively. Conscious breathing activates the parasympathetic nervous system, the body's natural mechanism for calm and restoration. As awareness expands through body scanning and interoception—the perception of internal bodily states—the mind shifts from survival mode to presence. This unified awareness quiets the default mode network, reducing anxiety and self-focused thought. In this stillness, breath and body are no longer separate from awareness—they become its expression.

How to Practice

Find position:

Sit or lie down comfortably. Allow your body to be supported by the surface beneath you. Take several slow, deep breaths—in through your nose, out through your mouth—letting tension begin to settle.

Notice the breath:

Without changing it, observe your natural breathing rhythm. Feel air entering and leaving the body. Notice how breath rises, expands, and falls on its own.

Scan the body:

Move your attention slowly from the crown of your head down through your face, neck, shoulders, arms, and torso—then to your hips, legs, and feet. Wherever awareness touches, allow that part of the body to soften.

Breathe into tension:

When you encounter tightness or discomfort, bring the breath to that place. Imagine each exhale creating space and softness. Let the breath move through the body like warm light, easing what is held.

Widen awareness:

Expand your focus to encompass the entire body. Sense the body as a single, living field of breath, weight, and warmth. Feel how breathing unites it all into one rhythm.

Rest in wholeness:

Let body, breath, and awareness merge into stillness. There is nothing to change or control. Simply rest in being—whole, grounded, alive.

Conclude the practice:

Take a final deep breath. Gently open your eyes, stretch if needed, and return to your surroundings, carrying the steadiness of that breath within you.

Twenty

Sensing Sound and Silence

Origin

From the opening words of creation myths to the chants of monasteries and temples, sound has always carried sacred power. In the Hebrew story of beginnings, the world unfolds through a voice: "Let there be." Across traditions, sound is understood as a bridge between spirit and matter—a vibration that calls form into being.

Silence, too, holds its own divinity. The prophets spoke of encountering the divine not in wind or fire but in the "still small voice." In mystical Christianity, silence was the space where divine presence could be perceived most clearly. Across faiths, seekers learned that creation and contemplation depend on the same rhythm: vibration and quiet, word and breath, sound and stillness.

For centuries, monks and mystics used chanting or humming not only as praise but as physiological preparation for silence. The vibration of the voice grounds the mind and centers awareness in the body. In the Christian desert tradition, repetition of short phrases—sometimes just a single tone—was said to quiet the inner noise until a deeper listening emerged.

Today, neuroscience affirms what these ancient practitioners discovered. Humming activates the vagus nerve, which regulates heart rate, breathing, and emotional balance. This stimulation engages the parasympathetic nervous system, reducing anxiety and promoting calm. Alternating between vibration and stillness creates what psychologists call rhythmic regulation—a pattern that synchronizes body and mind. The result is a quiet that feels alive, a silence still humming beneath the surface.

How to Practice

Settle the body and breathe:

Sit comfortably with your back upright and your body relaxed. Take several slow, deep breaths—in through your nose, out through your mouth—allowing the breath to steady and your awareness to gather.

Begin with sound:

On your next exhale, hum or chant a single note. Let the sound vibrate gently through your chest and throat. As you continue, notice all the places in your body where the vibration can be felt—perhaps in your ribs, jaw, sinuses, or even fingertips. Feel the resonance more than you listen to the tone itself. Continue for several breaths, allowing the sound to move through you like an inner current.

Enter silence:

When the tone fades, remain still. Notice the echo that lingers in your body—the quiet after the sound, the living silence beneath it. Rest in that space.

Alternate between sound and silence:

Continue in cycles—a few breaths of humming followed by a few breaths of silence. Let each phase lead naturally into the next. Don't force a pattern; follow what feels balanced.

Awareness of contrast:

Notice the relationship between vibration and stillness, sound and silence. Sense how one gives meaning to the other. Feel the body's calm deepen as the cycle continues.

Conclude the practice:

Let the final tone fade on its own. Sit quietly for a few breaths, resting in the peace that remains. Then open your eyes, carrying that quiet resonance with you.

Twenty-One

Expanding Compassion

Origin

This practice traces its roots to the ancient Buddhist discipline known as metta bhavana, a Pali phrase meaning "the cultivation of loving-kindness." In early Buddhist communities, it was considered essential training for awakening the heart. The practice invites the mind to turn again and again toward goodwill until compassion becomes not an emotion but a way of perceiving the world.

At its core, metta is the recognition that all beings share the same longing: to be free from suffering and to live with ease. The Buddha taught that this understanding begins with oneself and radiates outward in widening circles, to loved ones, strangers, and even adversaries. Over time, those circles dissolve into a single field of shared life.

Similar threads appear across traditions. The Hebrew prophets spoke of loving the stranger, Jesus urged love for enemies, and Sufi mystics described the heart as a mirror reflecting divine compassion for all creation. Each path returns to the same truth: that compassion is the language through which the sacred speaks in human form.

Psychologically, the effects of metta bhavana are profound. Studies in contemplative neuroscience show that cultivating compassion strengthens regions of the brain associated with empathy, particularly the insula and anterior cingulate cortex. This process of neuroplasticity retrains habitual responses to threat and fear, increasing patience, connection, and emotional regulation. Compassion practice thus becomes both spiritual discipline and neural transformation, reshaping perception itself.

How to Practice

Settle the Body and Breathe:

Sit comfortably with your back upright and your body relaxed. Take several slow, deep breaths, in through the nose and out through the mouth, allowing the breath to calm the body and soften the heart.

Begin with Self:

Silently repeat, "May I be safe. May I be peaceful. May I live with ease." Let the words move slowly, matching the rhythm of your breathing. There is no need to force emotion; trust the repetition to plant its seed.

Expand to Loved Ones:

Bring to mind someone dear to you. See their face, imagine their presence, and offer the same blessing: "May you be safe. May you be peaceful. May you live with ease." Notice any warmth or tenderness that arises naturally.

Include the Neutral:

Picture someone you neither like nor dislike, a passerby, a coworker, someone you barely know. Offer them the same words. Let the mind rest on their shared humanity.

Extend to the Difficult:

Bring to mind someone with whom you experience tension or pain. If resistance arises, acknowledge it gently and return to the breath. Offer the same wishes: "May you be safe. May you be peaceful. May you live with ease." You do not need to feel affection, only the intention to wish them well.

Universal Compassion:

Finally, expand awareness outward to include all living beings: "May all beings be safe. May all beings be peaceful. May all beings live with ease." Let the words dissolve into the vastness of that intention.

Conclude the Practice:

Allow the phrases to fade. Sit for a few breaths in quiet openness. Feel the warmth of compassion resting in the body. When ready, open your eyes, carrying that gentleness into the world around you.

Twenty-Two

Increasing Awareness

Origin

This practice parallels what the Buddhist tradition calls samādhi, a term meaning "to bring together" or "to unify." In early texts, it referred to gathering scattered attention into a single, spacious awareness. Rather than narrowing the focus to one object, this form of meditation expands perception until awareness itself becomes the field of contemplation. Everything belongs; nothing is outside the whole.

Similar currents appear in Christian mysticism, particularly in the contemplative reading of the phrase "In God we live and move and have our being." Early monastics and later mystics like Meister Eckhart spoke of God not as an external presence but as the ground of being in which all things exist. To rest in this awareness was to awaken to what is always already true: that separation is illusion.

In this practice, awareness unfolds like concentric circles—the body, the breath, the room, the world—each expansion revealing the same still center. The purpose is not to escape the world but to perceive its unity. Attention becomes less about what you notice and more about noticing itself—pure, open, inclusive.

Psychologically, this mirrors what neuroscientists call open monitoring, a state in which the brain's attentional networks expand to include all sensory input without judgment or preference. This kind of awareness reduces activity in the default mode network, associated with self-referential thought, while increasing theta wave coherence, linked to creativity and emotional balance. The result is an embodied sense of connection—spaciousness without detachment, presence without grasping.

How to Practice

Settle into posture:

Sit upright yet relaxed, with the spine tall and the body at ease. Take several slow, deep breaths, in through the nose and out through the mouth, letting attention settle into the body.

Notice the body:

Bring awareness to physical sensations—contact points, weight, temperature. Feel the solidity and support beneath you. As you move forward, continue holding this awareness of the body as the foundation of all that follows.

Notice the breath:

Observe the natural rhythm of your breathing. Sense the rise and fall, the subtle expansion and release within the body. Maintain awareness of both body and breath together as a single field of experience.

Expand to the whole body:

Widen awareness to include the entire body at once. Feel breath and body as one continuous presence—tingling, warmth, stillness—all included in awareness.

Expand to the space around you:

Without losing awareness of body and breath, sense the air brushing your skin, the space surrounding you. Feel the room's invisible volume meet the living space of your body.

Expand to the room:

Let awareness extend further to include the entire room. Without opening your eyes, include the walls, the floor, the ceiling, the sounds, and the quiet between them. Hold body, breath, and space together in one inclusive awareness.

Expand beyond:

Allow awareness to continue outward—beyond the room, into the building, the street, the trees, the sky. Each expansion includes everything from earlier expansions; nothing is left behind. Let awareness feel vast yet grounded, open yet embodied.

Rest in open awareness:

Rest here, where everything is included and nothing is separate. There is no center and no edge, only awareness aware of itself.

Return:

When ready, draw awareness gently back to the body and breath. Feel the contact points again, the weight of your body, the steady rhythm of breathing. Take one final deep breath and open your eyes, carrying the quiet vastness within.

Twenty-Three

Intentional Walking

Origin

This practice originates in the Buddhist tradition, where it is known as walking meditation or *cankama bhāvanā*—the cultivation of awareness through deliberate movement. In the Theravāda lineage, monks practiced it between long periods of seated meditation, using each step as a continuation of mindfulness rather than a break from it. In Zen, *kinhin* carries the same essence: slow, steady walking that synchronizes step, breath, and presence.

Walking meditation turns something ordinary into a teacher. Each step becomes a meeting place between body and earth, intention and surrender. Ancient teachers described it as mindfulness in motion—a way to carry awareness into the living moment, where gravity, breath, and attention align.

For many practitioners, the insight is simple but profound: every step is incarnation in motion—awareness made visible through the rhythm of the body. To walk intentionally is to experience how groundedness and grace coexist. The practice is not about the destination but about intimacy with each moment of contact between the foot and the earth.

In psychological terms, mindful walking cultivates sensorimotor integration—the brain's capacity to link movement, attention, and sensory feedback. Studies show it regulates the autonomic nervous system, improving balance and reducing anxiety by activating the parasympathetic response. As movement and awareness synchronize, the mind quiets. Attention settles in the body, and the body becomes prayer.

How to Practice

Prepare the path:

Choose a straight, quiet path about ten to thirty paces long. Indoors or outdoors, it should feel safe and free of obstacles.

Settle the body:

Stand tall but relaxed. Let your shoulders soften and your arms rest naturally. Take several slow breaths, feeling your weight distributed evenly through both feet.

Rest the gaze:

Keep your eyes open but unfocused, resting gently on a point a few feet ahead. Let sounds, sights, and sensations be present without grasping.

Set intention:

Silently affirm your purpose: "Walking to know walking." This is not exercise or travel but awareness in motion.

Begin slowly:

Move at half your normal pace. With each step, notice the sensations—lift, move, place. Feel the shifting of balance, the contact of foot with ground, the subtle flow of breath accompanying each movement.

Turn mindfully:

When you reach the end of your path, pause for one breath. Turn slowly, aware of the shifting weight and the pivot of the body. Then continue in the opposite direction with the same attention.

Meet distraction kindly:

When thoughts or emotions arise, acknowledge them silently—perhaps with the word "thinking" or "feeling." Then return to the rhythm of walking.

Adjust the rhythm:

If you grow dull or restless, slightly quicken your pace. If anxious or scattered, slow down. Let the tempo balance your mind.

Conclude with gratitude:

When finished, stand still for a moment. Feel the stability of the body, the breath, and the ground beneath you. Offer quiet thanks before resuming ordinary walking.

Twenty-Four

REFLECTING ON THE DAY

Origin

This practice comes from the spiritual tradition of St. Ignatius of Loyola, the founder of the Jesuits, who taught that awareness of the divine is found not in withdrawal from the world but in the midst of daily life. He called it the Examen of Consciousness—a short, structured reflection at the close of the day meant to help practitioners "find God in all things."

Unlike confession or analysis, the Examen was never meant to measure success or failure. It is an exercise in awareness—learning to see where life feels aligned and where it feels fragmented, where grace flows freely and where it is resisted. Ignatius described these inner movements as consolation and desolation: moments that draw us toward or away from love. Over time, he believed this daily noticing would teach discernment, helping the soul grow more responsive to the quiet currents of divine presence.

For those who do not frame experience in explicitly theistic terms, the same process remains deeply transformative. It can be practiced as an evening reflection that cultivates gratitude, emotional honesty, and intentional living. By noticing patterns in our reactions and values, we strengthen metacognitive awareness—the mind's ability to observe itself—and support emotional regulation, a key factor in resilience and wellbeing.

Psychologists note that such reflective practices activate the prefrontal cortex, balancing emotional centers of the brain and increasing clarity before rest. Whether seen as a prayer, a mindfulness exercise, or a daily self-audit, the

Examen invites the same awakening: to live with open eyes, noticing both light and shadow with compassion.

How to Practice

Become Present:

Sit comfortably and take several slow, deep breaths. Let your attention settle into the present moment. If it feels natural, invite awareness of the sacred—whatever that means for you.

Give Thanks:

Recall moments of gratitude from the day—large or small. Let appreciation arise for what nourished you: a conversation, a kindness, a quiet moment.

Review the Day:

Gently walk through the events of the day in sequence. Notice where your energy rose or fell, where peace deepened or tension grew. Pay attention to emotional shifts more than to details.

Face What Emerged:

Be honest about resistance, failure, or joy. Notice without judgment. If regret arises, hold it gently; if gratitude grows, let it expand. Both are teachers.

Renew Intention:

Turn toward tomorrow. Ask yourself what small, loving response might bring greater alignment or peace. Set a quiet intention rather than a resolution.

Close in Quiet:

Let the reflections fade. Rest for a few breaths in gratitude and peace, allowing the day to integrate before sleep or return to activity.

Twenty-Five

Centering Stillness

Origin

This practice comes from the spiritual tradition of St. Ignatius of Loyola, the founder of the Jesuits, who taught that awareness of the divine is found not in withdrawal from the world but in the midst of daily life. He called it the Examen of Consciousness—a short, structured reflection at the close of the day meant to help practitioners "find God in all things."

Unlike confession or analysis, the Examen was never meant to measure success or failure. It is an exercise in awareness—learning to see where life feels aligned and where it feels fragmented, where grace flows freely and where it is resisted. Ignatius described these inner movements as consolation and desolation: moments that draw us toward or away from love. Over time, he believed this daily noticing would teach discernment, helping the soul grow more responsive to the quiet currents of divine presence.

For those who do not frame experience in explicitly theistic terms, the same process remains deeply transformative. It can be practiced as an evening reflection that cultivates gratitude, emotional honesty, and intentional living. By noticing patterns in our reactions and values, we strengthen metacognitive awareness—the mind's ability to observe itself—and support emotional regulation, a key factor in resilience and wellbeing.

Psychologists note that such reflective practices activate the prefrontal cortex, balancing emotional centers of the brain and increasing clarity before rest. Whether seen as a prayer, a mindfulness exercise, or a daily self-audit, the

Examen invites the same awakening: to live with open eyes, noticing both light and shadow with compassion.

How to Practice

Become present:

Sit comfortably and take several slow, deep breaths. Let your attention settle into the present moment. If it feels natural, invite awareness of the sacred—whatever that means for you.

Give thanks:

Recall moments of gratitude from the day—large or small. Let appreciation arise for what nourished you: a conversation, a kindness, a quiet moment.

Review the day:

Gently walk through the events of the day in sequence. Notice where your energy rose or fell, where peace deepened or tension grew. Pay attention to emotional shifts more than to details.

Face what emerged:

Be honest about resistance, failure, or joy. Notice without judgment. If regret arises, hold it gently; if gratitude grows, let it expand. Both are teachers.

Renew intention:

Turn toward tomorrow. Ask yourself what small, loving response might bring greater alignment or peace. Set a quiet intention rather than a resolution.

Close in quiet:

Let the reflections fade. Rest for a few breaths in gratitude and peace, allowing the day to integrate before sleep or return to activity.

Twenty-Six

GUIDED BY VALUES

Origin

Across the world's spiritual traditions, people have discovered that repeating a simple phrase can quiet the mind and center the heart. In Hinduism, Sanskrit mantras like *Om Mani Padme Hum* are used to embody compassion. In Buddhism, the recitation of phrases such as *Namo Amitābha Buddha* opens awareness to infinite presence. In Islam, *dhikr*—the rhythmic remembrance of God's names—focuses the heart on divine unity.

Christianity, too, has its own form of mantra practice: the Jesus Prayer. Emerging among Eastern Orthodox monks in the deserts of Egypt and Palestine, it became the heartbeat of the Hesychast movement—a tradition of inner stillness and continuous remembrance. The prayer's rhythm, "Lord Jesus Christ, Son of God, have mercy on me," was repeated with the breath until the words sank beneath consciousness, transforming repetition into awareness. The goal was not endless recitation but unbroken attention—a life guided by love.

Modern adaptations of this ancient rhythm need not depend on theology. Any phrase that names one's deepest values—peace, compassion, forgiveness, love—can serve as a steadying point for awareness. The practice trains the mind to return, again and again, to what matters most.

Psychological studies of mantra meditation and contemplative prayer show that rhythmic repetition reduces self-focused rumination and activates neural pathways linked to empathy and emotional regulation. The pairing of breath and phrase also stimulates the vagus nerve, soothing the nervous system and grounding awareness. In both spiritual and scientific language, the result is the same: the breath becomes a vessel for meaning, carrying intention into stillness.

How to Practice

Choose a two-part mantra:

Begin by selecting a short phrase divided into two natural halves—one for the inhale, one for the exhale. Choose words that express a core value or truth you want to embody. Examples: Inhale: "Peace within." Exhale: "Peace around. "Inhale: "I receive love." Exhale: "I release fear." Inhale: "Lord Jesus Christ, Son of God." Exhale: "Have mercy on me."

Find stillness:

Sit comfortably with your back upright and your body relaxed. Take several slow, deep breaths, in through your nose and out through your mouth, allowing your breath to settle into a natural rhythm.

Align breath and phrase:

Silently pair the first half of your mantra with each inhale, and the second half with each exhale. Let the phrase move with the breath rather than trying to control it.

Let the rhythm deepen:

Continue for several minutes. When the mind wanders, simply notice and return to the breath and phrase. The practice is not about perfect focus but about returning—over and over—to what matters most.

Move from words to presence:

As repetition continues, the words may fade. Let their essence remain, a quiet resonance in the background of your awareness. Rest in the meaning they awaken.

Carry it into the day:

When you're ready, pause for a few breaths before moving on. Later, return to your phrase during moments of stress or pause—it becomes a compass, guiding you gently back to intention and calm.

Twenty-Seven

Deeper Messages from Texts

Origin

This practice, traditionally known as Lectio Divina, began among early Christian monastic communities as a way to move beyond analysis of scripture into a slower, more contemplative encounter with meaning. The Latin phrase translates to "divine reading," but here it is understood as deep listening, an invitation to let words speak to you rather than mastering them. Monks in the third and fourth centuries used this method to transform the act of reading into a form of meditation, where insight arose not through study but through stillness.

Over centuries, Lectio Divina spread beyond the monastery walls and evolved into a universal method for inner reflection. It appears in similar forms across traditions, from Buddhist repetition of sutras to the poetic recitations of Sufi mystics. Wherever people sought wisdom in words, they discovered that slow, repeated attention could reveal something beyond intellect. In this version, Deeper Messages from Texts, the same process is adapted for anyone seeking clarity or self-understanding, whether through sacred texts, literature, or personal writing.

This practice treats reading as savoring, not consuming information but tasting meaning. A phrase or word may shimmer or echo. The invitation is to linger with it, not to interpret too quickly, but to see what emotion or memory surfaces. In this quiet repetition, something unseen becomes visible.

Psychologically, this process engages associative thinking, the same mechanism that dreams use to weave memory and emotion into image. It also activates interoceptive awareness, the body's ability to sense its own state, allowing subtle emotional cues to surface alongside thought. Studies in contemplative neuroscience suggest that such focused, repetitive attention quiets the brain's default mode network, reducing self-narration and opening space for new insight. Whether understood as the subconscious offering wisdom or as the sacred whispering through words, the result is the same: a message emerges that feels both ancient and newly your own.

How to Practice

Settle the body and breathe:

Sit comfortably with your back upright and your body relaxed. Close your eyes, or soften your gaze. Take several slow, deep breaths, in through your nose and out through your mouth. Feel the weight of your body, the rhythm of your breath, and the stillness gathering around you.

Select a passage:

Choose a brief text that holds meaning for you, a line of poetry, a sacred verse, or even a sentence from a journal. Shorter is better; a few lines are enough.

Read the passage slowly, several times:

Read the text aloud, or silently, several times, each pass as slowly as possible. Let every word register. With each reading, notice which word or phrase keeps drawing your attention, or returns again and again. If more than one stands out, keep repeating the passage until a single word or phrase continues to shimmer for you.

Experience the shimmering word:

Set the passage aside. Take up the single word or phrase that keeps returning. Repeat it softly, aloud or inwardly, letting it float in awareness. Notice sensations, emotions, images, or memories that arise. Stay with experience, not analysis.

Ask and listen:

When you feel connected to the word, ask gentle questions: Why this word? What might it reveal to me right now? Let any awareness or memory come naturally.

Rest in silence:

Center your attention on the chosen word or phrase. As other thoughts arise, gently respond to each with your word, acknowledging the thought and letting it pass. Continue to breathe slowly, allowing the word to anchor you in quiet awareness until both word and thought dissolve into stillness.

Twenty-Eight

STRESS IN THE BODY

Origin

Modern psychology and ancient spiritual traditions agree: the body keeps score. Emotional experiences, especially stress, anxiety, and grief, do not just live in our thoughts; they manifest as tension, constriction, or heaviness in the body. The shoulders rise, the jaw locks, the gut tightens. Somatic meditation offers a way to listen to what the body is saying when words cannot. It is not analysis but awareness, an act of attention that turns compassion inward.

In spiritual terms, this practice honors the body as sacred ground. The incarnation affirms that the divine meets us not in abstraction but in flesh. The breath, muscles, heartbeat, and nerves are not obstacles to peace but the very channels through which it flows. To release tension is to cooperate with grace, to let love inhabit the body again.

Psychologically, this process helps re-regulate the nervous system. Breathing into areas of tension activates the parasympathetic nervous system, signaling safety and calming stress hormones. Research in somatic therapy and trauma recovery, particularly by psychologist Bessel van der Kolk and somatic educator Peter Levine, shows that gentle awareness and breath can release stored emotional energy and restore a sense of safety. Each cycle of focusing, breathing, and releasing gently rewires habitual patterns of holding, teaching the body that it is safe to relax.

Somatic meditation is thus both prayer and physiology: the practice of letting the body speak and listening until it sighs in relief.

How to Practice

Settle and center:

Find a quiet place to sit or lie down. Close your eyes or soften your gaze. Take several slow, deep breaths, allowing the body to settle and the breath to lengthen. Let your attention turn inward.

Name the issue:

Bring to mind a specific situation or thought that is causing stress or anxiety. It might be a conflict, a responsibility, or an uncertainty. Do not analyze; simply acknowledge.

Notice where it lives in the body:

Ask gently, "Where do I feel this in my body?" You might sense a tight chest, a knot in your stomach, tension in your jaw, or heaviness behind your eyes. "Stored" does not mean literal storage. It means the body is expressing emotional strain through sensation.

Breathe into that place:

Inhale slowly through your nose, imagining the breath reaching that area with light and softness. Exhale through your mouth, releasing what no longer serves you. Let the exhale be slightly longer than the inhale to cue relaxation.

Soften and release:

With each breath, imagine the area loosening, uncoiling, and opening. Notice warmth, tingling, or ease. If emotion arises, sadness, anger, or relief, let it move through without resistance.

Repeat three rounds:

After a minute or two, bring the same issue back to mind. Notice whether it still feels lodged in the same place or if it has shifted. Repeat the breathing and releasing process two more times, each round softening more deeply.

Rest in wholeness:

After the third round, let go of the issue entirely. Breathe naturally and sense the entire body as one unified field, alive, open, and grounded.

Integration:

End with gratitude for your body's wisdom. You might silently say, "I release what I no longer need. I honor my body for holding me through it."

Twenty-Nine

Guided Imagery

Origin

Guided imagery meditation is an ancient practice reborn in modern form, a meeting place of contemplation, psychology, and art. For millennia, spiritual traditions have used imagination not as fantasy but as revelation. The Hebrew prophets dreamed in symbols. Early Christian mystics spoke of inner landscapes filled with light, water, and voice. Buddhist and Sufi teachers guided students through mental imagery to awaken compassion and insight. Across these paths, imagination was never mere invention; it was a way of perceiving the inner world.

Modern psychology has rediscovered this wisdom. Techniques of guided imagery are used in therapy, stress reduction, and somatic healing to access what words cannot. When the mind pictures a scene with sensory detail, the nervous system responds as if it were real, heart rate slows, muscles soften, emotions surface. The practice invites cooperation between conscious thought and the subconscious, allowing deeper layers of memory, intuition, and emotion to speak.

In contemplative terms, guided imagery can be understood as entering prayer through symbol. The imagination becomes a sacred landscape where insight arises, not by force but by permission. The goal is not to create meaning but to let meaning reveal itself.

The next four chapters offer examples of this practice, meditations that use imagery to help the subconscious surface what most needs to be seen or healed. Each one leads the listener into a symbolic environment, a river, a room, a forest, a light, where intuition and grace can meet.

How to Practice

Prepare the space:

Find a quiet place where you can sit or lie comfortably. Dim the lights if possible. Take several slow, deep breaths to center yourself and release tension.

Set an intention:

Before beginning, hold a gentle openness to whatever may arise. You might silently say, "May I see what I need to see." The aim is not control but curiosity.

Engage the senses:

As you begin the guided meditation, allow your imagination to awaken. Notice what you see, hear, feel, and even smell within the imagery. Let the scene unfold without trying to direct it.

Pause for reflection:

Throughout these meditations, you will encounter questions or invitations such as, "What do you see?" "What do you hear?" "What happens next?" Each time, pause. Allow your imagination to fill in the scene, to make it concrete and alive. These moments are how your subconscious participates in the story, expressing meaning through symbols, sensations, and emotion. Do not overthink. Simply let whatever arises take form.

Follow what emerges:

When something in the image draws your attention, a sound, a path, a gesture, a light, follow it. Often these details are the language of the subconscious, offering symbols or memories that carry meaning.

Stay with the experience:

Resist the urge to interpret too soon. Let sensations, emotions, and impressions develop naturally. The meaning often becomes clearer after the meditation ends.

Return and reflect:

When the meditation concludes, take a few moments to breathe deeply and reorient yourself to the present moment. You may wish to write down what you saw, heard, or felt. Sometimes a single image or phrase continues to work quietly within you long after the practice ends.

Narratives for Guided Imagery

Thirty

A MESSAGE IN THE FOREST

You are sitting in a forest.

Comfortably.

It's a forest space that seems magical to you—the big trees, the way the air feels, even the smell.

Take a moment to breathe in.

Notice the smells that are there.

Name them. Not just a plant, but the nature of the smell.

Is it sweet? Sharp? (pause)

You feel the softness of the ground under you.

Pay attention to the weight of your body on the ground.

How does it feel underneath you? (pause)

As the air moves, notice your skin.

What parts of your skin feel the air first? (pause)

And then listen.

What do you hear?

What do you hear first? (pause)

As you listen closely, you begin to notice sounds that didn't rise above the others at first.

The more you listen, the more you hear. (pause)

This is a place you've come to over and over again in your life.

Not every day, not every week, but your whole life has memories connected to this spot.

It's late afternoon, and you can see the warm diversion of sunlight dappling through the trees.

You look up and see the familiar canopy—it lays over you like a blanket.

Pay attention to how it makes you feel.

The emotions that live in that space. (pause)

As you focus on those emotions, memories appear—like whispers. Like ghosts.

You can see the elementary school version of yourself.

What do you see that child doing?

Delighting. Unafraid. (pause)

When you were that age, you didn't come alone.

Who was there with you?

Who else do you see? (pause)

You sense that it's been too long since you came back to this place.

You remember the first time you came alone, just before you were a teenager—that sense of independence and freedom.

What did you do then?

What do you see? (pause)

You watch as that preteen version of yourself walks down a path, and you decide to follow.

You get up slowly.

What do you feel under your hands?

What does the ground feel like under your feet? (pause)

You walk slowly, deliberately.

Savoring the memory, not sure where the path leads.

As you follow, the forest gets thicker.

Darker.

More mysterious.

You look around and remember walking this path over and over again.

What emotions are you feeling now? (pause)

The air takes on a different quality—thicker, like it's drawing you in.

Wrapping around you.

You can feel your imagination coming to life. (pause)

You go farther in.

And just as it seems too dark to continue, you see sunlight in a clearing ahead, shining down like a spotlight. (pause)

You pause for a moment, not quite ready to leave the darkness.

Then slowly, you take another step.

You hear the ground beneath your feet.

What sounds does it make as you walk? (pause)

You're on the edge of the clearing—the tips of your toes just barely breaking the line where sunlight hits them.

And you see yourself.

The memory you've been following. (pause)

You remember that just beyond this spot, you had built something as a child.

And this preteen version of you is looking for it.

You follow.

And somehow, after all these years, you see the remnants.

You remember what it looked like.

What was there?

What had you built as a child, returning to it now?

How does it feel? (pause)

You enter that moment so many years ago.

You can feel what you felt then. (pause)

You see yourself as a child with your companion, building it for the first time.

Then the memories blow away into the forest.

You sit down, staring at the remnants of what you built years ago.

You pick up a piece.

It's almost as if touching it brings back wonderful emotions.

They wash over you as you feel the breeze move through the air. (pause)

You look up into the forest and remember—you found something one day, just a little farther down the path. (pause)

You don't see it.

You hear it.

Hints of a song.

A beat.

A melody you can't quite place. (pause)

You stand and follow the song—a song on the wind.

It's as if the wind itself is blowing you in the right direction. (pause)

You walk slowly, as if the younger versions of you are your companions.

Holding your hands.

Pulling you forward. (pause)

You can't remember what it was that you discovered.

But the younger versions of you can't wait for you to see it again. (pause)

Then you smell something—sweet and innocent.

You realize you're approaching the edge of this part of the forest. (pause)

Through the thick branches, you begin to see the outline of a building.

You have the sense you're stepping into a fairy tale.

You reach the edge of the woods and see it—not as it is now, but as the magical version you once imagined. (pause)

You remember the way flowers climbed the vines.

You remember tending them as a child. (pause)

And you see it as it is now.

It's as if no one has been here since you last came.

The vines have taken over, but it doesn't feel ruined.

They're covered in the most beautiful flowers. (pause)

You walk up and see the door covered with vines.

You slip back into the familiar rhythm, pulling the vines away.

Petals fall at your feet, as if the flowers themselves are creating a welcome mat. (pause)

You remember the way they felt on your bare feet—so you do it again.

You step onto the mat of petals.

How do they feel?

What sound do they make under your feet? (pause)

You open the door and walk in.

Each corner has a small altar—collections of things you once found important. (pause)

You turn to the right and pick up the treasure you left there.

What was it?

What was the magical thing? (pause)

You turn it over in your hands.

Then you notice a shining object out of the corner of your eye.

You walk toward it and pick it up.

What is it?

Why did you leave it there? (pause)

Then you remember—there was a hiding place.

You walk over, remove the cover, and find a folded piece of paper.

It says "To:" and your name, written in your childlike handwriting. (pause)

You can't touch it at first.

It has power.

It feels like it's pulsing.

It feels sacred. (pause)

You take deep breaths.

You know what's inside is important for you right now, though you can't remember what it says. (pause)

It feels as though the note is pulling your hands toward it, but you resist.

You stare at it—the color of your writing, the feel of the pen you used. (pause)

And somehow, that memory gives you permission.

You reach out, take it in your hand, but you don't open it.

You feel the weathered paper—dried, rippled from age. (pause)

You stand and walk out, carrying the note with you.

You're back in the forest, on the dark path toward the clearing. (pause)

You return to the remnants of what you built and sit down again.

Your younger selves are with you.

They're looking at you, waiting. (pause)

It's Christmas morning, and they can't wait to see you open it.

So you do.

Slowly.

You hear the paper as you unfold it.

You read the words—not many. Just one message.

What does it say? (pause)

You close your eyes.

You feel the warmth of the sun on your back.

And you're grateful. (pause)

Thirty-One

The Search

Imagine that you are in a house.

The house is not the one you live in now, but it is yours.

It's a big house, sitting on a lot of land.

Right now, you are sitting on a couch.

Pay attention to the way the couch feels on your legs and body.

Notice the smells—the good ones, the ones that make you feel at home. (pause)

You're feeling worried.

You've lost something.

Something important.

Something you need.

Something you have a deep connection with—and you don't know where it is.

You get up from the couch and begin to look.

Look around the room.

Notice the things that are there. (pause)

One by one, go to each thing.

Look around it.

You won't find what you're looking for, but you still search.

Take them apart in your mind—the furniture, the rugs. (pause)

Then you walk through a door into the kitchen.

There's a deep drawer full of all kinds of things.

You open it and begin to rummage through.

Pay attention to the things you pull out.

None of them are what you're looking for, but name them in your mind. (pause)

The funny thing is, you can't remember what it is that you're looking for—

but you know that when you see it, you'll recognize it. (pause)

You go downstairs into the garage.

Stand in the doorway and notice everything there.

No car—just piles of things.

Look at each one.

How does it smell? (pause)

You walk down the two stairs.

Notice how they feel under your feet. (pause)

You begin to look again, knowing that when you see it, you'll know—

but you won't find it there.

Then you remember the closet—the one with the shelves, the sheets, the medicine.

You leave the garage and go there.

As you walk, you cross through the rooms.

You feel the hardwood floor.

You hear it creak.

You feel the rugs and the carpet beneath you. (pause)

You turn the knob and open the closet.

What do you see there? (pause)

Take a moment.

Look piece by piece.

Notice what each thing feels like in your hands. (pause)

You still don't find it.

As you close the closet door, you realize— you know where it is,

even though you don't know what it is.

And it's not in your house.

You walk to the front door, noticing the smells,

the sound of your steps on the floor,

the sense of relief that you know where it is. (pause)

At the door, you pick up your shoes—

the ones you wear for long walks.

You open the door to a large porch with rocking chairs.

Notice the way it sounds. (pause)

The sun is out, but the air is cool.

You walk to a rocking chair, sit down, and put on your shoes.

You smell the wonderful outdoors. (pause)

In front of your house is a grassy field.

Beyond it—a forest.

You walk down the steps, hearing their sound,

and onto the sidewalk, noticing the difference in how it feels beneath your feet. (pause)

You walk out to the two-lane road in front of your house and cross it.

You begin walking through the grassy field.

The grass is deep enough that your shoes get lost in it.

Look down at your feet as you walk.

Notice the way the grass looks, the softness of the earth.

What do you hear? (pause)

You keep walking.

It's a long way through the grass.

Pay attention to the smell. (pause)

You're getting close to the forest.

You can see it's darker there,

but you know exactly where the gravel path begins. (pause)

As you get closer, the grass gets thinner.

You hear the difference between the sound of grass and gravel.

You step into the forest.

The gravel crunches under your feet. (pause)

Without the sun, it's cooler here.

The sounds are different.

Pay attention to them. (pause)

Keep walking the familiar path—the one you love.

You spot a favorite place, a tiny clearing with a large rock just right to sit on.

You stop.

You sit.

You feel the coolness of the rock under your hands. (pause)

Take deep breaths, soaking it in. (pause)

It's starting to be evening.

The forest is getting darker, but not scary.

The forest is the place you come to heal.

The place where you feel grounded. (pause)

But the thing you're looking for isn't here, and you know that.

So you get up and begin walking again,

noticing how the gravel is covered with leaves and branches.

The texture changes under your feet.

The sound changes. (pause)

You keep walking.

The path turns.

The forest is getting lighter.

You're nearing the other side.

Listen to the sounds.

Feel the cool breeze on your skin. (pause)

You reach the edge.

You can see another grassy area.

You can see the path turning back into gravel, winding up a hill.

You can't see over the top.

You leave the forest.

And just as you come out, you remember—

you still don't know what you're looking for,

but you remember it's in a gold box. (pause)

A gold box big enough to hold a softball.

A pasteboard box covered in gold glitter.

You keep walking.

Notice the gravel under your feet.

Notice how the sounds have changed. (pause)

You used to walk this path every day with someone you loved—someone who has passed.

You remember those walks.

It's not a sad memory.

It makes you deeply happy.

Who is that person? (pause)

You remember how, every once in a while,

they would reach out and give you a side hug as you walked.

You soak in that memory—every ounce of happiness and hope. (pause)

Then you feel a touch on your arm,

a side hug.

You look to your right, but no one is there.

And yet you know—they are walking with you.

In spirit.

In memory. (pause)

You smile.

You're halfway up the hill.

You stop.

You turn around.

You look back at the forest, the path.

You smell the air.

You feel the cool breeze.

You notice how the evening sun is changing the colors around you. (pause)

And you feel the excitement of knowing you're close.

So you turn and keep walking up the hill.

It doesn't make you tired.

You've walked this path a hundred times before.

You know the rhythm—the pace that keeps you breathing easy,

the one that lets you enjoy every step. (pause)

You reach the top of the hill and pause.

You stare into the grass beyond.

You squint, trying to see the glitter in the distance. (pause)

You can't quite see it.

It's just too far away.

So you begin walking again.

Down the hill now.

A gentle slope.

The path winds lazily downward.

Notice your feet.

Your skin.

The smell of the fresh air. (pause)

This is the moment in every walk when you become totally relaxed.

When the stress, the chores, the weight of life fall away.

When you are fully present in the walk. (pause)

You keep walking and see a small animal in the grass.

What is it? (pause)

It's wild, but not afraid of you.

It just watches you as you pass.

You imagine it has seen you every day of its life.

It treats you as another creature in the field. (pause)

You keep walking.

The path curves wide to the left.

And then, just to your right—you see it.

The box.

The gold glitter catching the light.

The lid resting on top.

You turn off the path and walk toward it.

The grass is higher here, but not uncomfortable.

Another small animal watches you pass, unafraid.

Notice how this grass feels different from the path.

Different from the other field. (pause)

You look up.

You start to feel excited.

The box is about ten steps away.

You count the steps slowly.

You stop. (pause)

The box is at your feet.

You look down—and pause.

You think about how strange it is that you can't remember what's inside,

but you do remember leaving it here.

You remember sitting in the grass,

deciding that this object needed to stay here for a while. (pause)

You reach down and pick up the box.

Notice how the glitter feels on your fingers. (pause)

You lift the lid.

You look inside.

What's there? (pause)

The velvet-lined box.

You take it out.

Hold it in your hand.

How does it feel? (pause)

Then you remember—there's an inscription.

You turn it so you can see the words.

What does it say? (pause)

And then you remember—there's something written inside the lid, too.

You pick it up.

You read it.

What does it say? (pause)

You sit down in the grass,

feeling the coolness on your legs,

the crisp breeze on your skin. (pause)

You take ten deep breaths,

sitting with the object,

feeling its meaning settle inside you. (pause)

Thirty-Two

THE DESERT GATE

You are standing barefoot in the sand.

Notice the ground beneath you—its warmth, its quiet give, the way it meets your weight. (pause)

Take a slow breath.

What do you smell? (pause)

Let your hearing open.

What sound reaches you first—the wind, the hush of shifting dunes, something alive in the distance? (pause)

Feel the air move against your skin.

Where do you notice it most?

Is it gentle, steady, playful? (pause)

Look toward the horizon.

What colors linger there?

What is the last light of day doing to the sand? (pause)

Find the rhythm between your breath and the wind.

Do they match? (pause)

A satchel rests against your hip.

You feel its strap beneath your fingers.

What texture do you notice?

How heavy is it?

Where in your body do you sense that weight? (pause)

Ahead, a gate rises from the desert—

its edges softened by sand and time.

You begin to walk toward it.

What changes underfoot as you move?

What rhythm forms between your steps and the wind? (pause)

With each breath, the air cools slightly.

Colors deepen—gold, rose, violet.

The gate grows taller as you approach. (pause)

Something moves beside you—

a small animal, its fur the color of the dunes.

It keeps your pace.

Its nearness feels familiar, natural.

Each time it glances your way, you feel a quiet comfort—

a reminder that you are not walking alone.

What emotion rises as you notice its company? (pause)

Behind you, soft steps join the rhythm of your own.

You don't turn.

The sound is steady, known.

A warmth settles at your side—

reassuring, calm, kind.

Your breath eases.

What does their presence bring into you? (pause)

The gate grows near.

Light gathers around it.

You stop.

The animal settles at your feet.

The air feels still, waiting. (pause)

You lift the satchel from your shoulder.

Notice the release in your muscles.

It leaves a small hollow in the sand. (pause)

Kneel and open it.

Inside are many things you've carried for a long time. (pause)

Reach in once.

What comes to your hand?

How does it feel?

What memory moves with it? (pause)

Watch as it begins to dissolve—

slowly, quietly—

edges softening, weight lifting,

until only the shape of its absence remains.

What changes in you as it disappears? (pause)

Reach in again.

Another object waits.

What is it?

What emotion rises with it?

Stay until it loosens.

Watch as it fades—grain by grain, light by light—

until it, too, is gone.

What remains in the space it leaves behind? (pause)

Reach in a third time.

A new shape meets your palm.

What moment does it hold?

Breathe through it.

Let it lighten.

Watch it dissolve into air,

leaving only calm in your hands.

How does that calm feel? (pause)

If one more remains, take it gently.

It feels warm—almost alive.

Hold it softly.

Let whatever it carries rise and pass.

Watch it fade—slowly, quietly—

until the warmth itself becomes air.

What do you feel in your hands now that it's gone? (pause)

Look inside.

The satchel is empty.

The wind moves through it,

lifting a few grains of sand.

Close the flap.

Set it beside you.

The sand begins to cover it.

What does that look stir within you? (pause)

The animal rises.

It circles once, then turns toward the gate.

You stand.

The air feels lighter now—easier to breathe.

The first stars appear. (pause)

You feel that familiar warmth again—

the quiet presence beside you.

It brings steadiness, reassurance, a sense of peace.

What part of you feels different because they are here? (pause)

Together, you walk toward the gate.

At its edge, you pause.

The animal slips through, unhurried.

The air tastes clean.

You breathe in.

What do you feel moving through you as you exhale? (pause)

You sense the presence beside you once more—

still here, gentle, constant.

Gratitude fills you.

What are you thankful for in this moment? (pause)

Take one last look at the desert behind you—

the wind reshaping the sand,

your footprints already fading.

What is the last thing you notice before you turn away? (pause)

Then you step forward through the gate.

Feel the air on the other side—its temperature, its stillness.

What changes in you as you cross? (pause)

The stars shimmer overhead.

Your body feels light.

You breathe once more.

The desert keeps your secret. (pause)

Thirty-Three

THE RIVER OF VOICES

You are sitting beside a river.

Notice the ground beneath you—cool, firm, alive with quiet sound. (pause)

Take a breath.

What do you smell? (pause)

Let another breath come.

What do you hear—the movement of water, the whisper of wind, something alive nearby? (pause)

Feel the air on your skin.

Where do you notice it first?

What temperature does it carry? (pause)

Look toward the water.

Its surface catches the light and lets it go again.

What colors move across it now? (pause)

You reach down.

Your fingers find smooth stones beneath the surface.

Cold. Solid. Grounding.

What does that texture awaken in you? (pause)

The sound of the water shifts.

A faint undertone rises—something like whispering, or maybe memory.

You listen.

What do you hear in it?

Words? Laughter?

Something you once knew? (pause)

The river seems to invite you.

You stand and begin to walk along its edge.

Each step changes the sound.

What rhythm do you hear now between your breath and the current? (pause)

The ground beneath you turns to soft earth and fallen leaves.

The air thickens slightly with the scent of growth.

What fragrances drift here?

What sounds come from deeper in the forest? (pause)

Light flickers through the trees.

How does it move across your skin? (pause)

The voices move with you—not louder, just closer.

You pause.

What do they sound like now?

Do you recognize any of them?

What feeling rises as you listen? (pause)

You keep walking.

The forest begins to thin.

The ground softens into reeds and mud.

You step into a marshy stretch where the river widens.

The air is heavy with moisture.

What scents reach you here?

What sounds emerge from this place?

What movement do you sense around you? (pause)

The river's voice changes—lower, slower, like a song sung half in dream.

You kneel beside it.

What color is the water now?

What does it reflect back to you? (pause)

Stay for a moment.

What emotion moves through you as you watch? (pause)

Then stand again and walk on.

The marsh gives way to meadow.

Grass bends beneath your steps.

What do you feel brushing against you as you walk?

What sounds carry across the open air? (pause)

The current grows stronger—fuller, almost choral.

You catch hints of words among the ripples,

but they shift before you can hold them.

The wind joins in, weaving through the grass.

What happens inside you as you listen? (pause)

You follow the river toward a bend ahead.

Light changes.

Air cools.

The sound gathers.

What do you sense waiting around the corner? (pause)

The river widens into a still, glassy pool.

You step closer.

Its surface mirrors the sky.

You kneel beside it.

Look down. (pause)

Your reflection looks back.

Then another.

And another—younger, older,

faces that remember,

faces that still wonder.

They shift and blur like ripples in time.

Which one meets your gaze?

What do you feel as you see it? (pause)

You lean closer.

The reflection speaks—

a message meant for this moment.

What does it say? (pause)

...

Listen.

The words drift away almost as soon as you hear them.

The ripples erase the images,

leaving only water and sky.

Watch as the current steadies again—

just water,

just flow.

What remains in you now? (pause)

Breathe in.

Cool air, full of stone and green and sky.

Breathe out.

How does your body feel as everything settles? (pause)

You stay there a while,

watching the calm return.

The voices have vanished,

but their peace lingers.

Where do you feel that peace resting? (pause)

You rise slowly.

The river moves beside you—quiet, silver, endless.

You walk a few steps back along its edge.

The air feels lighter.

The ground steadier beneath your feet.

Each step seems to echo with the same calm rhythm of the water. (pause)

You pause once more.

Look at the river.

It moves on without hurry.

What part of you moves with it?

What part of you stays still? (pause)

Inhale deeply.

Exhale fully.

The river carries everything away—

and you remain. (pause)

To contact Jeremy Steele for speaking engagements,
please visit jeremy-steele.com.

Many Voices. One Message.

quoir.com

www.ingramcontent.com/pod-product-compliance
Lightning Source LLC
Chambersburg PA
CBHW021126070726
47591CB00014B/1642